0-590-35489-2

Real Life Employment

Teacher's Edition

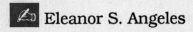 Eleanor S. Angeles

ISBN 0-590-35489-2

12 11 10 9 8 7 6 5 4 3 2   0/9

Printed in the U.S.A.

Teaching Guide

Contents

Introduction

Real Life Employment puts the learning of basic skills in the context of job situations: alphabetizing and categorizing as a file clerk, reading sales tax charts as a cashier, reading a road map as a gas station attendant, taking and writing messages as a receptionist, filling out a credit card form as a salesperson, and more. This program has been designed to teach the basic reading and writing competencies required of students both in school and on the job.

Real Life Employment is a developmental program that enables students to deal with basic skill learning in a practical and meaningful way. The program can be used by itself as an intensive language arts or job skills course for one-half to one full semester, depending upon the students' capabilities. It can also be used as an ongoing supplementary program that gives relevance to the academic curriculum.

The Program Components

The complete *Real Life Employment* program consists of:

- one book of 32 print masters and 8 visuals (overhead transparencies) to be used as pre-tests, follow-up skills practice, or post-tests;
- twenty copies, plus one desk copy of a 128-page worktext with skill instruction and practice in basic reading and writing tasks applied to specific jobs;
- one annotated Teacher's Edition with a teaching guide which lists specific skills objectives for each unit and suggests multi-level teaching activities for each lesson; and with answers to the student practice activities conveniently shown on the same pages where the activities are found in the worktext; and
- one 32-page Teacher's Guide for language minority students.

Using the Components

Print Masters and Visuals

Accompanying each of the eight units in the Skills Book are four print masters and one visual.

Print Master 1, for example, is a skills survey test to help you determine how much direct guidance the students will need in each of the lessons in Unit 1.

Print Master 2 has a matching visual and is useful as a springboard for class discussion of important skills and concepts taught in the unit.

Print Master 3 contains skill activities that relate to the visual.

Print Master 4 reinforces major skills and applies them to new situations.

A score of 80% or less in the skills survey tests (Print Masters 1, 5, 9, 13, 17, 21, 25, 29) is an indication that the student is not ready to work on the worktext independently. In this case, use the preparatory activities for each lesson as described later on in this guide.

Worktext	The 128-page worktext, to be used by the students for learning functional reading and writing skills, is divided into these eight units:
UNIT 1	**Job Hunting:** comparing and contrasting want-ads, writing a business letter, filling out an application, answering questions at an interview;
UNIT 2	**Working in Stores:** reading signs and categorizing, reading a price list, reading a tax chart, comparing labels, filling out a laundry ticket, using credit card forms;
UNIT 3	**General Office Work:** filing, sorting mail, reading directories, taking phone messages;
UNIT 4	**Specialized Office Jobs:** following directions to operate a copying machine, finding information, proofreading, keyboarding from dictation as a word processing operator, transcribing with correct punctuation and capitalization, using the Yellow Pages;
UNIT 5	**Service Jobs:** knowing road signs, giving directions from a road map, reading a menu, recognizing cause and effect in first aid, outlining sequential directions for hair styling, writing specific travel information;
UNIT 6	**Working with Your Hands:** using diagrams, reading special charts, knowing the tools used by a carpenter, drawing conclusions in appliance repair, inferring the cause and effect of a simple plumbing job;
UNIT 7	**Government Jobs:** reading postal rate table, remembering definitions and terms in the armed services, using reference materials, finding main ideas and detail (in written material) as a firefighter, writing a factual report as a police officer;
UNIT 8	**New Jobs/New Technology:** reading job descriptions, reading a floor plan, putting data in the right sequence, picking out interview facts.

Every two-page lesson in the worktext has the following elements:
- A statement of the lesson's purpose;
- A list of the skills used in the lesson;
- Words to Know;
- Tips on acquiring important job skills;
- Developmental activities and exercises that gradually lead to the attainment of the unit objectives.

The review exercises at the end of each unit are divided into three sections:
- Vocabulary;
- Reading;
- Writing.

Annotated Teacher's Edition	The 32-page guide at the front outlines the set of objectives for each unit and provides specific teaching suggestions for the attainment of these objectives. It describes the preparatory activities necessary for students who do not pass the skills survey test. It suggests implementation techniques and follow-up enrichment exercises. The answers to the practice exercises are on the same pages where they are found in the student worktext.

Unit 1
Job Hunting

Objectives

The student will demonstrate the ability to:
1. read, compare, and contrast want ads;
2. correctly write a business letter in response to an ad;
3. correctly and legibly fill out job application forms; and
4. give relevant answers to questions posed during a job interview.

Skills Survey

Print Master 1 surveys the skills used in Unit 1. Results of this test will help you determine how much direct guidance the students will need from you. An 80-100% accuracy is an indication that the student can work independently on this unit.

Introducing the Unit

Go over the Table of Contents on page 5 in the worktext so that every student knows what will be covered in each lesson. This provides an opportunity for group work in case you choose to let each student work independently on the lessons.

Lesson 1 | Help-Wanted Ads
(worktext pp. 6-7)

Preparatory Activities

For students whose skills survey tests show that they are not ready to begin work in Unit 1, use the following activities:
1. Study the classified ads in today's newspaper. Make a list of the abbreviations used in the ads and fill in their meanings.
2. Choose two ads for the same type of job. How are the ads alike? How are they different? List their similarities and differences.

Class Discussion

Establish the pattern of the lessons by calling attention to the opening paragraph, Words to Know and how-to tips. Point out that big numbers are always followed by specific directions on how to do the exercises.

If the students have reading problems, orally read page 6, and the top of page 7 with them. Then help them work out the first few items of each activity.

Additional Activities

1. Collect the want-ad sections of five consecutive issues of the same newspaper. Note where new jobs are inserted. Which job ads were taken out after two issues? When do more jobs seem to be advertised?
2. Make a list of benefits that are available from different employers. Choose three that you think would be most important to you. Tell why.
3. Choose three positions that are advertised with the annual or yearly salary shown in the ad. Find out how much they would pay by the week and by the month.

Lesson 2 | In Response to Ads
(worktext pp. 8-9)

Preparatory Activities

1. Locate and write down the correct business address of at least three companies where you might choose to work.
2. Locate two ads in the newpaper that ask for a response by letter. List the information they require and note their complete addresses.
3. Look for a sample business letter and identify its parts.

Class Discussion

Discuss the parts of a business letter, calling attention to the punctuation marks, capital letters, position of different parts, and spaces between parts. Explain why failure to follow the basic format could cause the applicant to lose a job opportunity. Also note that this format applies to all types of business letters.

Additional Activities

1. Write a letter in response to an interesting ad that you have seen in your local newspaper. Compare it with the letter on page 8. Be sure to include all seven parts of a business letter.
2. Tell why a correctly written business letter would be more important to someone applying for a secretarial position than to someone applying for the position of elevator operator.
3. List three appropriate closings for a business letter. List three that are suitable only for a friendly letter.

Lesson 3 | Forms About You
(worktext pp. 10-11)

Preparatory Activities

1. Check your written work in the previous lessons. Is your writing neat and clear? Do all your letters slant in the same direction? Do the letters have the same height? Are the words evenly spaced? If not, practice writing on lined paper until your handwriting is neat and readable.
2. List the facts about you that you think might be required on every job application form.

Class Discussion

Stress should be placed on the Tips given in the lesson. In extreme cases of illegible handwriting, a remedial handwriting workbook should be provided.

Additional Activities

1. Visit a local employment agency. Most of them will be glad to give you an application form to take with you. Compare and contrast their form with the one on page 11 of your worktext.
2. For each piece of information required on an application form, write why an employer might want it.
3. Try to get other forms that you must fill out to get a job. Fill out the forms neatly and accurately.

Lesson 4 | The Interview
(worktext pp. 12-13)

Preparatory Activities

1. What is the first thing you notice when you meet someone for the first time? Ask this question of yourself and of five other people. List the answers.

2. Tell how you might dress to apply for the job of: secretary to the owner/manager of a downtown family restaurant.

3. List the things you should do and shouldn't do during a job interview.

Class Discussion

You might begin this lesson by asking several students to describe their best friend or the person they admire most. What traits seem to predominate in all descriptions? Does this tell anything about the way employers judge applicants? Discuss the relevance of these traits (for example: honesty, neatness) to on-the-job situations.

Additional Activities

1. Find out what three documents can be used to prove your age. Your school library should have information that will help you find out.

2. Find out the origin and purpose of having a social security card. Make a report to the class.

3. Ask your guidance counselor to tell you how to get working papers that may be required in your state.

Unit Review | Vocabulary/Reading/Writing

(worktext pp. 14-16)

At the end of the unit are three tests to help you evaluate mastery of the skills and concepts taught so far. To remediate remaining weaknesses, help the students go back to the specific lessons that teach the skills. Alternative exercises and follow-ups are provided on Print Masters 2, 3, and 4.

Unit 2
Working in Stores

Objectives

The students will demonstrate the ability to:
1. read signs, categorize items, and give directions as well as follow them;
2. locate specific information while reading a price list;
3. locate information on a sales tax chart and apply that information correctly;
4. compare and contrast product labels;
5. correctly fill out claim tickets, using abbreviations;
6. correctly fill out credit card forms, using abbreviations when needed.

Skills Survey

Print Master 5 surveys the skills used in Unit 2. Results of this test will help you determine how much direct guidance the students will need from you. An 80-100% accuracy is an indication that the student can work independently on Unit 2.

Introducing the Unit	Due to the vast number of jobs available for sales clerks, and because of the fast turnover of employees in this field, it is perhaps one of the easiest job markets to enter. However, explain to the students that it is important to have some basic skills in order to obtain and retain this kind of job. Discuss the Introduction and Table of Contents on page 17 before proceeding to Lesson 1.

Lesson 1 | Stock Clerk
(worktext pp. 18-19)

Preparatory Activities

1. Look at the supermarket aisles on page 18. List some items that might be found in aisles 1A and 2A.
2. Study the floor plan of the drugstore on page 19. Name five items which might be labeled *Cosmetics*. Tell what items might be grouped on a counter labeled *First-Aid Supplies*.

Class Discussion

Call attention to the opening paragraph and Words to Know. Discuss the Tips and make sure the students know exactly what to do in the exercises.

Additional Activities

1. Make a floor plan of your local supermarket. Indicate where categories of goods are located.
2. Name as many local stores as possible that should stock shoe polish.
3. Suppose you have mastered the skills taught in this lesson. Name five other jobs that require these skills. Explain how each job uses a specific skill.

Lesson 2 | Bakery Sales Clerk
(worktext pp. 20-21)

Preparatory Activities

1. What is a price list? Why would a store post a price list? Name at least three stores that have a posted price list.
2. How is the price list at a bakery the same as that in a menu? How are the two different?
3. Look at the price list on page 20. List the categories you find.

Class Discussion

Have the students compare and contrast the bakery selection on page 20 with their neighborhood bakery. What items are unique in their bakery?

Ask questions to determine whether the students can locate specific items on the price list without difficulty.

Additional Activities

1. Suppose you have $10.00 to spend in the bakery. List as many different combinations as possible, using the chart on page 20.
2. Why is it easier for the employee behind the counter if a price list is posted? List as many reasons as you can.
3. What other job skills can you learn in a bakery? List at least five.

Lesson 3 | Cashier
(worktext pp. 22-23)

Preparatory Activities

1. Find out the rate of sales tax effective in your community. What items are taxable?
2. What does a cashier do? What kinds of machines might be used by a cashier? Name at least three.
3. Find out the difference between a sales tax and an income tax. Your school librarian can help you locate this information.

Class Discussion

Make sure that all students know the correct tax rate for their community. Even within some states the tax rate varies. Explain the range of amounts that have the same tax.

Additional Activities

1. Select five items from the list of bakery items on page 20 of your book. Total the items and figure the tax using your local sales tax.
2. Do all the exercises on page 23, using the current tax chart for your city. If it is the same as that on page 23, add 8¢ to the amount listed in each instance and then figure the answers.
3. In each store you buy from, see if the sales tax chart is posted and where it is located.

Lesson 4 | Hardware Store Sales Clerk
(worktext pp. 24-25)

Preparatory Activities

1. List 10 items that might be found in a hardware store. How could they be categorized?
2. Take labels or directions from several items that have been purchased at a hardware store. Use these labels to determine size of packaged items and their use. If the price is marked on the item, figure the sales tax and add it to the cost of the item.

Class Discussion

Stress the importance of comparing product labels. Discuss the basics and particulars described on page 24. Make sure the students understand the directions before allowing them to work independently on page 25.

Additional Activities

1. Go to a hardware store and find out how many different kinds of wrenches are sold there. What are their uses?
2. See if you can name five different units of measurement used in hardware stores. Name one item that is sold using each unit of measurement listed.
3. Using your local telephone directory, find out what stores stock exterior house paint. Compare and contrast at least two brands.

Lesson 5 | At the Cleaners
(worktext pp. 26-27)

Preparatory Activities

1. Why do cleaners issue tickets to customers? Give at least two reasons.
2. List at least 10 abbreviations that might be used on a dry-cleaning ticket.
3. Stop by the local cleaners and ask for a ticket. Tell them that you need it for class. If they are not too busy, they might take time to tell you some of the kinds of work they do.

Class Discussion

Explain that while abbreviations are a kind of shorthand, they should be easily read. Abbreviating is a useful skill because most forms to be filled out have limited space. Go over the Tips, pointing out that periods are usually left out when abbreviations are used on forms.

Additional Activities

1. Write out a ticket for five items of clothing you might take to the cleaners. Use abbreviations.
2. Why do you think some dry cleaners advertise one-day service? What are the advantages to the customer and to the store?
3. Suppose you have worked for a dry-cleaning store. What other jobs are you qualified for? Name at least three.

Lesson 6 | The Salesperson
(worktext pp. 28-29)

Preparatory Activities

1. List five credit cards that are accepted nationwide. Name several local businesses that issue their own credit cards.
2. Stop by a gas station and pick up an application for a credit card. What information are you expected to provide? Why do you think this information is required?

Class Discussion

Go over the information on page 28. Familiarize students with the terms used on credit card forms.

Additional Activities

1. What is the unit cost of 10 items if the total amount is $10.00? $12.50? $20.00?
2. Credit cards usually cost you some money. Find out how credit card companies earn money by lending it to you.
3. List at least five skills that are helpful to a salesperson. Describe how a salesperson might use each skill.

Unit Review | Vocabulary/Reading/Review
(worktext pp. 30-32)

The three end-of-unit review pages may be used as tests to determine what skill areas need more work. Additional exercises and follow-up materials are provided on Print Masters 6, 7, and 8.

Unit 3
General Office Work

Objectives

The student will demonstrate the ability to:
1. alphabetize words and names as necessary to establish and maintain files in an office;
2. categorize items which must be filed;
3. sort all incoming mail by floor, department, or addressee;
4. sort all outgoing mail, as well as use a zip code directory, and learn to properly package and address mail;
5. read a street map and a building directory and follow directions in locating certain points within a city;
6. answer a telephone properly, give information, and record details.

Skills Survey

Print Master 9 surveys the skills used in Unit 3. Results of this test will help you determine how much direct guidance the students will need from you. An 80-100% accuracy is an indication that the student can work independently on this unit.

Introducing the Unit

Use the Table of Contents on page 33 to preview the unit lessons. Point out to the students that while they may plan to be file clerks or office messengers rather than mailroom clerks, there are valuable skills to be learned in each lesson. Discuss how useful these skills can be in dealing with real-life situations. For example: "Why should we know how to take a telephone message, even if we don't plan to be a receptionist?"

Lesson 1 | File Clerk – Alphabetizing
(worktext pp. 34-35)

Preparatory Activities

For students whose skills survey tests show that they are not ready to begin work on Unit 3, use the following activities:
1. Have students alphabetize the names of classmates.
2. Using any family name, have the students alphabetize the names of at least five family members.
3. Using the Words to Know from the first three units in their book, have students make an alphabetical listing. (Do not be concerned with definitions at this point.)

Class Discussion

Lesson 1 focuses on using the alphabet in establishing and maintaining a file system in an office. Before turning to page 34, have the students suggest all the reasons they can think of for listing words and names. Their ideas might include such reasons as rosters for football or basketball teams, class roll, telephone directory, etc. Discuss why it is easy to locate the words in the dictionary. Have the students read the introductory paragraph after the heading *File Clerk*. Make sure they understand the skills they will be using in the lesson. Discuss the Words to Know. Go over the format of practice exercises 1 and 2 on page 35 before allowing the students to work independently.

For students who are able to do the lessons but show a need for more practice, use the following activities.

1. Using the Yellow Pages of a telephone directory, have the students select a company name from each of the following categories and tell in what order they would appear in the white pages.

_____ bakery   _____ plumber   _____ printing
_____ auto repair   _____ sporting   _____ electronics

2. Practice alphabetizing to the seventh letter. Example: accord, accorded, according, accordingly.

3. Give company names to be alphabetized. Example: R. C. Cola Company, M&M Candy Company, D. H. Holmes Co, Q&Q Oatmeal Company, S. & H. Green Stamp Co.

Lesson 2   File Clerk — Categorizing
(worktext pp. 36-37)

Preparatory Activities

1. If you were to file your school notes, what categories would you use?
2. Name at least five files that might be found in almost every office.
3. Group the following names into categories: Dwight Gooden, Ronald Reagan, Grover Cleveland, Willie Mays, Jackie Robinson, Fernando Valenzuela, John F. Kennedy, Abraham Lincoln. What are the categories?

Class Discussion

Discuss the Tips for filing by category. Explain why, in a chronological file, the most recent item appears first. Make sure the students understand the tasks required before letting them work independently on exercises 1-3.

Additional Activities

1. Tell whether the items in each folder should be filed alphabetically or chronologically: customer list, invoices, checks, personnel records, letters.
2. Name at least five files that might be found in each of the following businesses: bank, dental office, magazine publisher, travel agency.
3. Interview someone who works in an office. Ask about his or her filing system and report it to the class.

Lesson 3   Mailroom Clerk — Sorting Mail
(worktext pp. 38-39)

Preparatory Activities

1. Look at the employee directory on page 38. Group the departments by floor. Then group the employees by department.
2. Describe how you might sort the mail if you work in the mailroom of a large company.
3. There are two departments that are located on the 4th floor according to the directory on page 38. Why do you think these departments are together?

Class Discussion	Go over the methods used in sorting incoming mail. Ask questions to determine the students' ability to locate information in the employee directory.
Additional Activities	1. Give at least two reasons why fast delivery of mail is essential in a business office. 2. Decide which department might receive the following mail: a job application, a package of new reference books, a bill, a customer's complaint. 3. If you have worked as a mailroom clerk in a private office, are you qualified for a job at the Post Office? Why?

Lesson 4 | Mailroom Clerk — Handling Outgoing Mail
(worktext pp. 40-41)

Preparatory Activities	1. Most telephone directories have a zip code map. Using a local telephone directory, determine how many zip codes are used in your town. 2. Is the zip code directory arranged alphabetically or numerically? Why is it organized this way?
Class Discussion	Discuss the importance of zip codes. Have the students give reasons why mail should be properly addressed and packaged.
Additional Activities	1. Using a zip code directory, have students locate the zip codes for the following cities: Billings, Montana; Englewood Cliffs, New Jersey; Greenwich, Connecticut; Wheaton, Illinois; Destin, Florida; Houston, Texas; San Diego, California. 2. Have students find and list all the zip code numbers for Harrisburg, Pennsylvania. 3. Locate and list the correct abbreviations for these states: California, Maine, Montana, Illinois, Louisiana, Missouri, Mississippi. 4. Interview a Post Office worker. Ask what might happen if a letter is mailed with a wrong state abbreviation and a missing zip code.

Lesson 5 | Office Messenger
(worktext pp. 42-43)

Preparatory Activities	1. Find a street map of your town. Locate the Post Office, the fire station, and the supermarket. Which one has an even-numbered address. Which ones have odd-numbered addresses? 2. Where can you find a building directory? How is it used? 3. On what floor can you find each of these room numbers: 632? 1409? 122? 1729? 799? 333? 976? 1219?
Class Discussion	Before proceeding to the exercises on page 43, make sure each student can read a street map. Ask questions to determine if the students can locate names and floors on the building directory on page 42.

Additional Activities	1. Study the street maps of two towns. How are they alike? How are they different?
	2. Since some office messengers are required to drive a truck to deliver parcels and letters, use the map on page 43 to determine the best route to take for exercise 1 (d), if Kensington Avenue is one way going north and 9th Street is one way going east.
	3. What other jobs require the same skills that office messengers must have?

Lesson 6 | Receptionist
(worktext pp. 44-45)

Preparatory Activities

1. Name some qualities that a good receptionist has. (Answers might be: pleasant voice, good handwriting, neat appearance.)
2. What are the most important details in a message? Why?
3. Pretend that a call came in for your friend while he/she was out to lunch. Make up a telephone message.

Class Discussion

Go over the tips for getting and recording details. Discuss the importance of correct and complete information, especially in a business situation.

Additional Activities

1. The receptionist at the insurance company asks for your policy number whenever you call. Why do you think she needs that information?
2. In addition to taking telephone messages, the receptionist must often place long distance calls. Using your telephone directory, find the following information: area code for Dallas, Texas; how to dial an 800 number; and what the letters WATS stand for.
3. If there were no receptionists in an office, who would be responsible for taking telephone messages?

Unit Review | Vocabulary/Reading/Writing
(worktext pp. 46-48)

At the end of the unit are three tests to help you evaluate mastery of the skills and concepts taught so far. To reteach remaining difficulties, go over the specific lessons with the students. Alternative exercises and follow-up lessons are also provided on Print Masters 10, 11, and 12.

Unit 4
Specialized Office Jobs

Objectives

The student will demonstrate the ability to:
1. read a diagram as necessary to follow directions for operating office machines;
2. proofread typewritten work to find spelling and grammatical errors and correct them;
3. identify sound-alike words and use the correct word to fit the context of the sentence;
4. divide words into syllables and recognize prefixes and suffixes when used;
5. capitalize and punctuate business letters;
6. locate and evaluate information found in display ads of the Yellow Pages.

Skills Survey

Print Master 13 surveys the skills used in Unit 4. Results of this test will help you determine how much direct guidance the students will need from you in the unit lessons. An 80-100% accuracy is an indication that the student can work independently on this unit.

Introducing the Unit

Although the unit presents jobs that require special training, the skills used are those that all students should master in school. Let the students preview the Table of Contents on page 49. Elicit from them how the skills might be used in other situations.

Lesson 1 | Copying Machine Operator
(worktext pp. 50-51)

Preparatory Activities

1. Find a picture of an office machine. Try to name its parts and describe how it works.
2. Look at the two diagrams on pages 50 and 51 of your Skills Book. How are they alike? How are they different?
3. Draw a diagram of a stereo system and write simple instructions for operating it.

Class Discussion

Have the class list reasons for needing a copy of a document. If any student has made a copy using a machine, have him or her tell how it's done. Stress the importance of carefully reading and following directions.

Additional Activities

1. Find out what a copy would look like if the lever was too far on the dark side. What if it was too far on the dark side? What if it was too far to the light side?
2. Make a list of the kinds of machines used in an office. How many can you operate?
3. What damages can you cause by not following directions? Describe a situation to illustrate the importance of following directions carefully.

Lesson 2 | Word Processing Operator — Proofreading

(worktext pp. 52-53)

Preparatory Activities

1. There are five errors in each of the following sentences. Correct them.
   a. he come home jest in time to ate dinner?
   b. What do you no about The man jack was talking too.
2. Identify six common punctuation marks. Give an example of how you would correctly use each mark.

Class Discussion

Stress the importance of using a dictionary while proofreading. If the students do not know all that a dictionary can tell them, now is the time to see that they acquire the knowledge.

Additional Activities

1. See if you can find an error in a newspaper or a book. It's rare, but it does happen.
2. Copy a paragraph from a textbook as rapidly as you can. Then copy it a second time, slowly and carefully. Proofread the two copies. How many mistakes did you make on the first copy? How many errors did you find on the second copy?
3. Name at least five jobs that require good proofreading skills.

Lesson 3 | Word Processing Operator — Typing from Dictation

(worktext pp. 54-55)

Preparatory Activities

1. Write the homonyms for the following words: *hear, hair, to, there, so, no, new. fore, bear.*
2. If you have a tape recorder, have a friend tape a paragraph for you to write or type. When you finish writing from dictation, check your work for spelling, punctuation, homonyms, and capitalization.

Class Discussion

Dictate some sentences to the class to find out just how adept they are at listening, spelling, and writing. Give them time immediately after the dictation to use the dictionary and to correct their errors.

Additional Activities

1. Find out what antonyms and synonyms are. Will they cause problems for someone who takes dictation? Explain your answer.
2. What is a dictaphone machine? How does it work? You might ask someone who is currently using the machine on the job. You can also find information about the machine in the library.
3. Write a business letter using the homonyms you have learned in this lesson.

Lesson 4 | Word Processing Operator — Finding Information
(worktext pp. 56-57)

Preparatory Activities

1. Make a list of skills you use in school that will be useful when you get a job as a word processing operator.
2. List five types of information and indicate the best source for each (e.g. the telephone number of a business school — Yellow Pages).

Class Discussion

Discuss why being able to use reference materials is essential in word processing. Read page 56 with the students. Then have them work independently on the exercises on page 57.

Additional Activities

1. Use the Yellow Pages to find names of companies who might use word processors. List at least five companies.
2. Compare a typewriter with a word processor. List their similarities. List their differences.

Lesson 5 | Stenographer
(worktext pp. 58-59)

Preparatory Activities

1. What skills are useful to a stenographer? Name at least three important skills.
2. Name five punctuation marks and describe where each one is used.
3. List 10 words that are always capitalized.

Class Discussion

While this section will not teach those specific skills necessary for taking shorthand, it does teach the importance of learning school skills that are useful in such a job situation. Go over the skills to be covered as well as the words the students should know. Then let the students proceed independently.

Additional Activities

1. There are four kinds of sentences. What kind of punctuation should be used at the end of each sentence? Write one sentence of each kind.
2. Make a list of at least five words which are not usually capitalized when used in a title or heading.
3. Why is shorthand an important skill? Describe at least three situations where shorthand is essential.

Lesson 6 | Secretary
(worktext pp. 60-61)

Preparatory Activities

1. Using the Yellow Pages of your local telephone directory, locate and list the names of an exterminator, an appliance repair service, a moving company, and an optician.
2. Your boss has given you the job of buying a new desk and chair for his office. Look in the Yellow Pages for places to call. List several possibilities.

Class Discussion	This lesson could be a good opportunity for a classroom contest of finding the telephone numbers and addresses of certain businesses. Use the Yellow Pages, of course.
	Discuss the information supplied by the display ad on page 60.
Additional Activities	1. If you want to have the office coffeemaker repaired, you would look under *Appliances — Service and Repair*. How many places have display ads in your Yellow Pages? Which one would you call? Why?
	2. List other duties that a secretary might have. Name the skills that would be useful in performing these duties.
	3. Study the White Pages of your telephone directory. How is it different from the Yellow Pages?

Unit Review

Vocabulary/Reading/Writing

(worktext pp. 62-64)

These end-of-unit exercises may be used to evaluate mastery of the skills and concepts taught. Additional exercises and follow-up lessons are provided on Print Masters 14, 15, and 16.

Unit 5
Service Jobs

Objectives	The student will demonstrate the ability to:
	1. match symbols with their meaning in reading and following road signs;
	2. read a road map and give directions from it;
	3. understand vocabulary used in reading a menu;
	4. determine cause and effect, draw conclusions and predict outcomes while reading about first aid;
	5. understand, summarize, and outline sequential directions;
	6. distinguish between general and specific as is necessary for writing to give specific information.
Skills Survey	Print Master 17 surveys the skills used in Unit 5. Results of this test will help you determine how much direct guidance the students will need from you. An 80-100% accuracy is an indication that the student can work independently on this unit.
Introducing the Unit	As the students preview the unit, let them discover that the focus is on practicing important reading and writing skills. Specifically, practice will be aimed toward recognizing cause and effect, drawing conclusions, summarizing, outlining, and writing clear sentences — skills which are valuable in everyday real-life situations.

Lesson 1 | Chauffeur
(worktext pp. 66-67)

Preparatory Activities

1. Draw the shapes and symbols of several road signs that you pass on your way to school.
2. Give the highway number of the interstate highway that comes closest to your home. Tell where you might go if you took one of the routes.
3. Find a city map and a state map. How are they alike? How are they different?

Class Discussion

Go over the Words to Know, then let the students proceed independently. Most will be familiar with the road signs even though some may not be driving yet.

Additional Activities

1. Make a list of road signs which apply to pedestrians. Draw the shapes and the symbols.
2. Using a map of the United States, chart a route from Miami, Florida to San Francisco, California. Tell which interstate routes you would use. If you must travel on a road which is not an interstate highway, give its number also.
3. Make a list of highways near your town. Tell whether they are east-west routes or north-south routes. Give the highway number for each route.

Lesson 2 | Gas Station Attendant
(worktext pp. 68-69)

Preparatory Activities

1. Make a list of tasks a gas station attendant must perform. Name at least five things you are sure he must do.
2. Make a list of any toll roads within your own state. If your state has no toll roads, check a map of states bordering your state to see if you can locate the closest one.
3. Write down directions for someone who wants to locate your town on a state map. Do not use coordinates given on the map you use since the other person may not have the same map.

Class Discussion

This lesson teaches skills which so many people lack: reading a road map and giving directions. Many people lack those skills simply because they are not observant of things around them. This is a good time to begin developing observation and map-reading skills.

Additional Activities

1. Find and describe in some manner the points located on the following coordinates using a map of the United States: C6, E4, F3.
2. Find out what symbols are usually used for state parks, airports, or historical landmarks.
3. Using a state map and a map of the United States, compare the scale in miles and kilometers.

Lesson 3 | Food Server
(worktext pp. 70-71)

Preparatory Activities

1. What items are almost always found on a menu?
2. See if any local restaurants have copies of menus that they give to customers. Many restaurants which have take-out service do this in order to save time with telephone orders. Bring some copies to class to compare prices.
3. What are your favorite foreign dishes? Can you pronounce their names?

Class Discussion

Let the students use the dictionary to look up the pronunciation of the foreign words on the menu. Ask them if they know of other common dishes that have foreign names. What are these dishes and where did they originate?

Be sure the students can read the menu before allowing them to work independently on page 71.

Additional Activities

1. Fill out a check for the items you would choose from the menu on page 70. Fill out the charges as if you had ordered *a la carte.* Compare that to the dinner charge. What would be your best buy?
2. What is the most expensive dinner item on the menu? Why do you think it is more expensive than *Beef Goulash*? Give reasons for your answer.
3. What other jobs are available in a restaurant? Identify the skills required for each job.

Lesson 4 | Home Health Aide
(worktext pp. 72-73)

Preparatory Activities

1. List some traits you believe a home health aide should possess. Which of these traits do you possess? Do you think this is a job you would do well? Why?
2. What first-aid rules do you know? See if there is a book on first aid in your school library. Learn at least one new rule today that might help you or someone near you.
3. What are the causes and effects of a headache? The causes and effects of common cold?

Class Discussion

While this lesson touches on home health aides and their jobs, the real skill developed is that of drawing conclusions after determining cause and effect. Being able to predict the outcome is also called for, but not emphasized. The ability to think before acting is a result of using these skills wisely.

Discuss the Tips and facts on page 72 before allowing the students to work independently on page 73.

Additional Activities

1. Using the First Aid Basic Facts on page 72, tell the first thing you should do if someone is injured.
2. When would you move an injured person? Give two examples of times when an accident victim should be moved. Use complete sentences.

3. Tell about an accident you have witnessed. What was done to help the victim? Tell whether something else might have been done if everyone there had been familiar with first-aid rules.

Lesson 5 | Hair Stylist
(worktext pp. 74-75)

Preparatory Activities

1. Bring the directions for using some hair products to class. If possible bring the ones enclosed in the products. Compare these directions with those brought by classmates. Which products have simple directions? Which ones give detailed sequential steps?

2. Which do you think might have more detailed instructions included — a shampoo or a hair coloring product? Why?

3. Give an example of sequential directions for making something. List at least five steps in sequence.

Class Discussion

This would be a good time to review a skill learned in the previous lesson — determining cause and effect. What might happen if an important step in sequential directions is left out? Perhaps some of the students have had experiences they could share. After discussion along these lines, go over the Tips for Outlining Complex Directions. Then let the students proceed independently.

Additional Activities

1. Copy the sequential directions from a box of cake mix. Compare with those directions brought by other students.

2. Using the information provided on page 74 about *Honey Plus*, tell why you think the product would not be effective if you applied the yellow liquid to the hair as the first step.

3. What other service jobs are related to personal grooming? Identify the skills needed in each position.

Lesson 6 | Travel Agent
(worktext pp. 76-77)

Preparatory Activities

1. What information would you need to know before you leave to meet a friend who will be arriving at a large airport? Give your reasons for needing specific information.

2. Write a sentence that gives some general information about the weather in your town this week. Now write a sentence telling exactly what the temperature was — one particular day of the week.

3. Bring in brochures or other information about trips to various places. (Most bus companies or airlines usually have these brochures available to the public.) Between taking a bus or taking a plane, which would you prefer? Why?

Class Discussion

Whether you are a travel agent, a secretary, or just an individual about to go on a vacation trip, you must be aware of specific information that will be needed in order to avoid delays, etc. Make sure each student can distinguish between general and specific information. When specific information is given, make sure that the student understands the importance of the Tips given on page 76.

Additional Activities

1. Cut out magazine ads for vacation trips. Choose one trip which you might want to take. If possible, call an airline agent to find out the total cost of the trip, what meals are served, and any other useful information.
2. Give reasons why it might be important for a traveler to know what transfers are included in the cost of a tour package.
3. Go to the school library and find some information about codes. Why are they used? Can you invent your own code?

Unit Review | Vocabulary/Reading/Writing
(worktext pp. 78-80)

These end-of-unit exercises may serve as tests to determine mastery of the skills and concepts taught in Unit 5. Additional exercises and follow-up activities are provided on Print Masters 18, 19, and 20.

Unit 6
Working with Your Hands

Objectives

The student will demonstrate the ability to:
1. read and interpret diagrams;
2. follow directions as necessary in using a diagram or pattern;
3. read and follow directions on a flow chart;
4. compare, contrast, and draw conclusions as to what tool to use for a specific job.

Skills Survey

Print Master 21 surveys the skills used in Unit 6. Results of this test will help you determine how much direct guidance the students will need from you. An 80-100% accuracy is an indication that the student can work independently on this unit.

Introducing the Unit

Many students have the talent necessary for jobs covered in this unit. The unit therefore provides a good opportunity for the teacher as well as the students to see where their (students') real interests lie. Often, it might be the first opportunity for the student to display his skills to peers. Take advantage of this unit to get to know the real person behind each desk. Before proceeding to Lesson 1, go over the introduction and Table of Contents on page 81 of the student's book.

Lesson 1 | Oil or Gas Burner Mechanic
(worktext pp. 82-83)

Preparatory Activities

1. Bring to class a picture or diagram of any machine or equipment that you are familiar with and can operate.
2. Name the parts in the picture or diagram. Tell the class what you think are the important parts of the machine that make it work.
3. Describe to the class how, from your own experience, you operate the machine or equipment.

Class Discussion

Many homes use the type of heating described in this unit. However, many students will never see a unit of this kind. You may find it desirable to have a resource person from your community come into the class to discuss differences in kinds of heating used in homes. However you choose to teach the unit, the basic skills do not depend on the student having seen this type of heating unit. Go over the Words to Know, because the vocabulary in this unit will be more specialized than in most words in other units.

Additional Activities

1. Find out from the maintenance worker at your school or apartment building how the building is heated. If you live in a house, find out all you can about the heating system.
2. Make a list of all the parts labeled on the diagram on page 82 of your book.
3. Compare the parts labeled on page 82 with those of another piece of equipment. Which parts are not common to both machines?
4. Draw a diagram showing the path taken by electrical current from the source of origin in your home through a switch to a light. Your school library will have a book which can give you all the information you may need.

Lesson 2 | Garment Worker
(worktext pp. 84-85)

Preparatory Activities

1. Name all the jobs you can think of that have to do with the clothing industry.
2. Tell why you think it would be necessary to know something about how clothes are made if you intend to sell clothes in a department store.
3. If you have a sewing machine in your home or know someone who does, find out all the uses that the owner makes of it.

Class Discussion

There may be those in your class who have never seen a pattern such as those used to make clothes. Perhaps one of the students or the home economics teacher in your school could bring one to class and explain its use. The use of specialized vocabulary is necessary in all the lessons of this unit. Go over the Words to Know section. The students should understand that there are definite skills involved in the jobs studied in this unit that the worker may not know at all when hired as an apprentice.

Additional Activities	1. Bring a pattern to class and show the class examples of the symbols found on page 84 in your book.
	2. Bring a piece of material used in making a garment. Show examples of basting, bias, grain, selvage, etc.
	3. Do you think it would be more difficult to make a man's suit or a woman's dress? Give reasons for your answers.
	4. Use a pattern to make something. This need not be clothing. It may be made from wood, plastic, etc. Share it with the class.

Lesson 3 | Auto Mechanic
(worktext pp. 86-87)

Preparatory Activities

1. Name as many parts of an automobile as you can. Check the dictionary to see if you have spelled them correctly.
2. Find out if it is necessary to be an auto mechanic to get a job at a gas station. Share your finding with a friend.
3. Look under the hood of a car. If you don't have a car, go to a service station. See if you can recognize the radiator, horn, and carburetor.
4. Tell the class a few things about cars that people who drive should know so that they can be prepared to make repairs.

Class Discussion

Discuss the importance of knowing enough about any equipment you operate. Even if you call an auto mechanic to repair your car, it is important to know and to say where or what seems to be the trouble. Many times we can save ourselves costly repairs by being able to read a chart and follow directions. Go over the Tips on page 86. These Tips are useful guides to reading a flow chart correctly.

Additional Activities

1. Make a flow chart which might be used to diagnose a problem you are familiar with. It need not be as lengthy as the one on page 87.
2. Using the chart on page 87, make a list of things to do in case the horn relay does not click.
3. Look up the following words in a dictionary. In case of several meanings, give the one which is relevant. (a) circuit, (b) fuse, (c) switch, (d) ground, (e) short.
4. Name three things you might do before calling a repair person in case the light in your room doesn't switch on.

Lesson 4 | The Builder
(worktext pp. 88-89)

Preparatory Activities

1. The plans, patterns, or diagrams that a builder uses when constructing a house have a special name. Find out what these plans are called and, if possible, bring a copy to class.
2. Make a list of tools you are familiar with — that are used by a builder.
3. Name several tools every homeowner should know and should be able to use.

Class Discussion	Although this lesson deals basically with the tools used by a builder, the class may benefit from naming the tools of other trades. This will give those who are interested in other areas an opportunity to participate. To compare and contrast will be interesting when looking at the tools of different trades. This is a good time to practice categorizing also. Go over special vocabulary that is needed for the successful completion of the lesson.
Additional Activities	1. Which of the fasteners shown on page 89 would you use in each of the following cases? (a) putting trim on cabinet doors; (b) putting a license plate on a car; (c) hanging a picture on a paneled wall. 2. Name at least two other kinds of saws and tell how they are similar and how they are different. 3. A carpenter uses a tool called a plane. Draw a simple sketch of it and list its uses. 4. Select a tool used in some trade and demonstrate its uses to your class.

Lesson 5 — Appliance Repairer

(worktext pp. 90-91)

Preparatory Activities	1. Write down the names of all appliances used in your home. Are all of them run by electrical current? 2. If the food in your freezer is thawing, what would you do before calling an appliance repairer? 3. Look on your refrigerator door at home to see if there are suggestions as to what to do if the appliance does not seem to be operating properly. Write them down to share with the class.
Class Discussion	Stress the importance of drawing conclusions by going over the opening paragraph on page 90. Read the Tips for Drawing a Correct Conclusion. Then allow the students to work independently on page 91.
Additional Activities	1. Bring a wind-up alarm clock to school and demonstrate that Ms. Gleason's clock problem as given on page 91 of your book may be due to the fact that she has not read her operating instructions carefully. 2. Talk with an appliance repairer. Find out what special training, if any, is necessary before working with appliances. 3. Make a list of safety rules to observe in working with or on appliances. Use complete sentences.

Lesson 6 — Plumber

(worktext pp. 92-93)

Preparatory Activities	1. Name some tools used by a plumber. Are any of these the same tools used by a carpenter? Which ones are not? 2. Name some reasons for calling a plumber to your home or office. 3. What do you think could cause a faucet to drip? What are some possible effects of a dripping faucet?

Class Discussion	Go over the opening paragraph and the Words to Know. It would be advisable to carefully go over the Cause and Effect section at the bottom of page 92. Give more examples of cause and effect.
Additional Activities	1. Demonstrate a simple plumbing repair job to the class. You may use actual plumbing objects or equipment or an illustrated chart.
	2. Look up definitions for the following words. Give the relevant definition. (a) *washer*, (b) *stem*, (c) *threads*, (d) *valve*, (e) *pressure*.
	3. Make a list of other cause and effect relationships which have to do with plumbing problems.

Unit Review | Vocabulary/Reading/Writing

(worktext pp. 94-96)

These three end-of-unit exercises may serve as tests to check mastery of skills and concepts taught in Unit 6. Additional exercises and follow-up activities are provided on Print Masters 22, 23, and 24.

Unit 7
Government Jobs

Objectives	The student will demonstrate the ability to:
	1. read rate tables such as those used by postal workers;
	2. understand and remember terms and definitions;
	3. use reference materials to obtain facts quickly and accurately;
	4. read for main ideas, as well as supporting details;
	5. use own words to state facts and opinions;
	6. write a factual report.
Skills Survey	Print Master 25 surveys the skills used in Unit 7. Results of this test will help you determine how much direct guidance the students will need from you. An 80-100% accuracy is an indication that the student can work independently on the unit exercises.
Introducing the Unit	Establish the correlation between the skills used in the classroom and those required in government jobs. Discuss the unit introduction and the Table of Contents.

Lesson 1 | The Postal Service Worker
(worktext pp. 98-99)

Preparatory Activities

1. How many 25¢ stamps can you get for $15.00? $8.00? $2.50? $10.00?
2. How much postage is required on a half-ounce letter sent first class? What is the current rate for airmail letters?
3. Does it cost more to send a letter overseas? How much more? You can get this information from the Post Office.
4. Write a letter to a friend. Before you mail it, stop by the Post Office and have the letter weighed and stamped. Report your findings to the class.

Class Discussion

Before letting the students proceed with the lesson, be sure that everyone can read the rate tables. Some special vocabulary is necessary for the lesson, so go over the Words to Know.

Additional Activities

1. Using one of the rate tables on page 98, find out if a plant weighing one pound can be sent from Chicago to Portland by third-class mail.
2. Can you include a personal letter inside a 10-oz. book which you are sending by third-class mail? What would be the cost of mailing the book? Check with the Post Office before giving your answer.
3. Write a report about Express Mail. The information window at your Post Office is a good place to start your research.

Lesson 2 | Armed Services
(worktext pp. 100-101)

Preparatory Activities

1. Make a list of at least five common terms that come from military jargon.
2. Name at least one other occupation that uses the military clock as a method of telling time.
3. Go to the nearest Armed Forces Recruiting Office and collect brochures. Put them in a folder for use as a reference file.

Class Discussion

The class might categorize words used by special groups. This will provide an opportunity for some group participation and will give a change of pace from the routine of working independently.

Additional Activities

1. Make a list of jargon used by you and your friends. Give the meanings of each word listed.
2. Translate the following sentences: (a) Hit the deck! (b) It's chow time! (c) I must scrub the deck of the mess hall.
3. Do some research on why the military clock is used instead of the clock most people are familiar with. Write your report using complete sentences.

Lesson 3 | Information Expert
(worktext pp. 102-103)

Preparatory Activities

1. Name at least two current and reliable encyclopedias which you have used or have seen in your school library.

2. Name five kinds of information which can be obtained from an atlas.

3. Why do you think a cookbook might be considered a reference book? Compare and contrast it with an encyclopedia.

Class Discussion

Emphasize the importance of learning how to use reference materials to locate information. Most facts can be obtained from reference books quickly and accurately if one learns which reference to use for a specific purpose. Since most people have access to a public library, information is available to everyone.

Additional Activities

1. Using the most recent almanac, locate and list the number of square feet, the number of square yards, and the number of hectares in one acre.

2. Use the almanac or an encyclopedia to find the following information about a state that borders the one you live in: (a) state motto; (b) population; (c) year it entered the Union.

3. What book would you use to find out how fast an elk can run? Report your answer in class.

Lesson 4 | The Firefighter — Finding Main Ideas and Details
(worktext pp. 104-105)

Preparatory Activities

1. Why do you think firefighters should try to educate the public about fire prevention?

2. What is an arsonist and what is the penalty in your state for arson?

3. What can you do to prevent a fire? Make a list of at least five fire-prevention rules.

Class Discussion

Read over page 104 with the class. Discuss actual facts as presented in the report by the Fire Department of Scarsdale, NY. Let students proceed to page 105 independently.

Additional Activities

1. Bring an illustration or diagram of a smoke detecting device. Explain how it works.

2. Make a vocabulary list of jargon used by a firefighter. Get some help on this from a local firefighter.

3. How does the job of a forest ranger compare with that of a firefighter? Which job would you prefer to do?

Lesson 5 | The Firefighter — Saying Information in Your Own Words
(worktext pp. 106-107)

Preparatory Activities

1. Select an article from the newspaper. Read this article carefully so that you can tell it to the class in your own words. Don't forget to include all the main ideas.

2. Find the fire-alarm boxes near your school, home, and the place where you work. Read the directions for operating the fire alarm systems. Report to class about their locations and whether they all give the same operating instructions.

3. Give examples of facts. State some opinions about these facts.

Class Discussion

It is important to be able to state facts as well as give your opinion. It is most important that the students learn to separate the two so that it is clear which is fact and which is opinion. In order to determine if they can do this, some class time might be devoted to giving oral practice sentences.

Additional Activities

1. Plan an escape route for everyone in your family. Mark the routes on paper as suggested on page 107. Practice this several times to be sure everyone knows what to do.
2. Tell the class how to build a campfire and be sure to include details for extinguishing the fire.
3. Find out what kinds of fires can be put out with water, and what chemicals to use on other fires. Write your report. Be sure to separate facts from opinions. Tell where you got your information.

Lesson 6 | The Police Officer
(worktext pp. 108-109)

Preparatory Activities

1. Make a list of tasks that you think police officers perform.
2. Find out how much police officers, who are new on their jobs, make in your town. Find out too if they must go to a police training school and for how long. List some requirements for the job.
3. List some dangers involved in police work. List some advantages in this kind of work.

Class Discussion

Discuss why writing skills are essential to police work. If possible, have your class attend a court session or have an officer come to your class to talk with the students. Go over question words and their value in getting facts. Let students then proceed independently.

Additional Acitivities

1. Interview a local police officer. Find out the normal (legal) procedures they take when a suspect is apprehended.
2. Compare the forms they use to record facts with the form in your book.

Unit Review | Vocabulary/Reading/Writing
(worktext pp. 110-112)

These end-of-unit review exercises may be used to evaluate mastery of the skills and concepts taught in the unit. Additional exercises and follow-up lessons are provided on Print Masters 26, 27, and 28.

UNIT 8
New Jobs/
New Technology

Objectives

The student will demonstrate the ability to:
1. know his or her own abilities and interests;
2. read and interpret job descriptions;
3. read a floor plan;
4. put data in the right sequence;
5. distinguish fact from opinion.

Skills Survey

Print Master 29 surveys the skills used in Unit 8. Results of this test will help you determine how much direct guidance the students will need from you. An 80-100% accuracy is an indication that the student can work independently on this unit.

Introducing the Unit

Review the different kinds of jobs encountered in the previous units. Have students enumerate other jobs that they know. Discuss the unit introduction on this page and preview the unit lessons.

Lesson 1 Electronics Technician
(worktext pp. 114-115)

Preparatory Activities

1. Make a list of items that have been made possible by the science of electronics (e.g., television, radio, computer).
2. List some of the things that someone who works in electronics might do.

Class Discussion

Discuss why being good with one's hands and having good eyesight might be important characteristics to have when one works as an electronics technician. Read page 114 with the students. Then have them work independently on the exercises on page 115.

Additional Activities

1. Use the Yellow Pages to find names of companies who might employ electronics technicians. List at least five companies.
2. Interview an electronics technician. Then write his or her job description.

Lesson 2 | Computer-Aided Drafter
(worktext pp. 116-117)

Preparatory Activities

1. List five tasks that you could do better and faster with a computer.
2. Draw a map of the clasroom. Measure the area carefully.

Class Discussion

Go over the job description with the students. Explain each item if necessary. Then point out that the floor plan on page 117 is a drawing that a computer-aided drafter might do on a computer. Allow students to work independently on page 117.

Additional Acitivities

1. Draw a floor plan of your home.
2. Make a list of other jobs that require artistic ability.

Lesson 3 | Computer Operator
(worktext pp. 118-119)

Preparatory Activities

1. Think about the places you visit every week. List the places that have a computer.
2. Briefly describe a computer. You may want to visit a computer lab to give your description more details.

Class Discussion

Read page 118 aloud with the class. If necessary explain every item in the job description. The activities on page 119 may prove difficult for some students. Offer help when necessary.

Additional Activities

1. Make a list of businesses that employ computer operators.
2. Call or write a technical school and ask for the names of courses one takes when studying to be a computer operator.

Unit Review | Vocabulary/Reading/Writing
(worktext pp. 120-122)

These three end-of-unit exercises may serve as tests to check mastery of the skills and concepts taught in Unit 8. Additional exercises and follow-up activities are provided on Print Masters 30, 31, and 32.

Real Life Employment

Eleanor S. Angeles

Revision Supervision	ZIGG-LYN Publishing Concepts and Services Inc.
Illustrations	Norman Green, Laleine Gonzales
Cover Design/Production	Taurins Design Associates NYC
Cover Photograph	Ron Morecraft

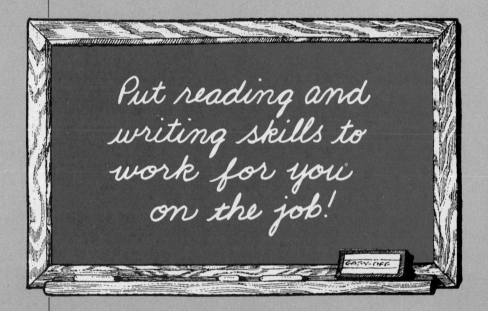

Grateful acknowledgement is made to Scholastic Inc. for excerpts from *New Jobs, New Technology* by Diane Storin, reprinted by permission of the publisher. Every effort has been made to obtain permission to use previously published material. Any errors or omissions are unintentional.

ISBN 0-590-35489-2

12 11 10 9 8 7 6 5 4 3 2   0/9

Printed in the U.S.A.

Contents

Introduction

In the eight units that follow, you'll find answers to these questions — and more. At first, you will search, apply, and interview for a job. Then you will apply reading and writing skills at work in different stores and offices. You will also experience doing service jobs and working with your hands. You will even have a chance to work for Uncle Sam! Finally, you will learn about new jobs created by new technology.

Throughout this book, you will learn and practice those reading and writing tasks that are actually performed in job situations. The skills can be used in various types of work. Following directions and filling out forms, while essential to the job hunter, are required skills for thousands of jobs. Alphabetizing, a skill used most often by file clerks, is useful to stock clerks and mail clerks as well. Proofreading, a typical skill for typists, is important to sales people too. Reading maps and road signs, a vital skill for truck drivers, is used by messengers, gas attendants, and just about every person who has to be on the road. Taking notes and writing messages are required skills not only for receptionists and secretaries; company presidents and managers use them too.

Unit 1

Job Hunting

Job hunting can be quite a job in itself. You must be able to put reading and writing skills to work for you. You have better chances of getting a job if you can read want ads, write a business letter, fill out forms, and answer the interviewer's questions correctly. Working in this unit does not guarantee a job for you. But when you're finished with the exercises, you will have a better idea of your job hunting skills.

Help-Wanted Ads

Comparing and Contrasting

You have an idea of your skills and interests. You think you know what type of work you would like to do. You also know that the newspaper can help you find the job you want. Now it's time to see how the newspaper lists and describes jobs you may apply for.

Words to Know

Appt	**Appointment** — time to meet
Exp	**Experienced** — did the same job before
Pref'd	**Preferred** — wanted
Rel	**Reliable** — can be trusted
Sal	**Salary** — pay
Temp	**Temporary** — short-term

How to Read Help-Wanted Ads

In the classified section of the newspaper, ads for similar kinds of work are usually grouped together. For example, you'll find ads listed under headings such as "Sales" or "Clerical" or "Mechanic." After you find the heading you're interested in, look at the ads listed.

Ads use abbreviations or shortened forms of words. Use context clues in the same ad to figure out the meaning of an abbreviated word.

How much would you be paid each week?

$250

In two words, write the kind of work you would do.

repair typewriters

Fringe benefits are the extras you get, such as paid vacations.

Do you have to pay for uniforms in this job?

No

They prefer that you have some natural talent in working with machines. Do you think you do?

Yes or no

How would you apply?

Call for appointment after 10 a.m.

SECRETARY/$300

Typing 50 wpm
1 year exp

Lots of room for
advancement

Two-week vacation
Exc. benefits

Call for interview
555-4444

Job A

SECRETARY/$360

Min 3 years
secretarial exp

Neat and accurate
typing skills 60+ wpm

Steno pref'd but not
required. Good phone
manner a must.

**Send resume to Jones Co.,
110 Main St.**

Job B

Compare and Contrast

When looking through the classified section, you may see more than one ad for the same kind of work. Carefully read the information in each ad. Then see how the salaries, hours, benefits, etc., are alike. See how they are different.

---

1. Write your answers on the lines.

a. In the two want ads above, which job pays more? _____Job B_____
How much more? _____$60 more_____

b. Which job promises that you can get ahead? _____Job A_____

c. For which job would you most likely use the telephone? _Job B_

d. To get job B, how much more experience is needed — than required for job A? _____two more years_____

e. For which job would it be helpful to know steno (shorthand writing)? _____Job B_____

2. Put a check (✔) in the box next to the best answer.

a. To apply for job A, you shoud first

❑ write for an appointment.

☑ telephone.

❑ come in for an interview.

b. To apply for job B, you should first

❑ write a letter.

❑ phone the company.

☑ send in your resume.

c. How do the jobs compare? How are they *alike*?

❑ They pay the same salaries.

❑ They both have good benefits.

☑ They both require previous experience.

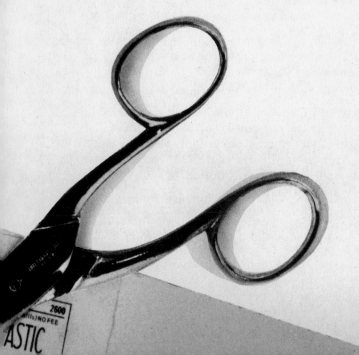

7

In Response to Ads

Writing a Business Letter
A help-wanted ad does not always tell you all the facts about a job. Sometimes, the only way to learn more about the job is to write for a personal interview. Your letter could open or close the door to a job. The door is more likely to open if you know how to write a correct business letter.

Tips for Writing a Business Letter

● Include all of the seven parts shown in Len O'Brien's letter:

A Your return address with the zip code

B Date

C Inside address (full name of the person or firm you are writing to, followed by a double space)

D Greeting followed by a colon (If you know the person's name, use Dear _____:. If not, use Dear Sir/Madam:.)

E The body or content of the letter

F A brief and formal closing followed by a comma

G Your typed or printed name and your signature above it

● Your letter should be polite, clear, and to the point.

● Your letter should be clean and neat. All words should be spelled correctly.

(A) 1722 Russell Circle
Colorado Springs
Colorado 80915

(B) May 20, 1982

Miss Pat Dalton
(C) P.O. Box 99
Pueblo, Colorado 81009

(D) Dear Miss Dalton:

In answer to your advertisement for a child-care worker in last Sunday's Newstime, I would like to apply for the position. I am 18 years old and about to graduate from Bradley High School.

At present, I am working part-time at the Bradley
(E) Child-Care Center. My supervisor there is Mrs. Betty Jackson.

I plan to work full-time after graduation and would like to learn more about caring for children. I am sure I could do a good job for you as a child-care worker. May I have an interview at your convenience? If you decide to call me, my telephone number is 555-2274.

(F) Sincerely yours,

Len O'Brien
(G) Len O'Brien

8

1. Len O'Brien's letter is an answer to this ad. Suppose you want to apply for the same job. First, answer the questions below. Then write or type your own business letter on a separate piece of paper.

a. What is your complete address?

(Answers will vary.)

_____

_____

_____

b. When are you writing this letter? _____ *today's date* _____

c. To whom should you address the letter? Include the name and address.

Miss Pat Dalton

P.O. Box 99

Pueblo, Colorado 81009

d. How should you write the greeting? _____ *Dear Miss Dalton:*

e. Why are you writing? Write the first sentence of your letter. *I would like to apply for the position of child-care worker.*

f. What closing will you use? How will you write it? *Truly yours, Respectfully yours, or Sincerely yours*

2. What information should you put on the envelope? Write the return address and the address on this envelope.

(Student's Address)

Miss Pat Dalton
P.O. Box 99
Pueblo, Colorado 81009

Forms About You

Filling Out an Application
The way you fill out forms tells a lot about you. A complete, neatly written application shows that your work will be as neat and complete. Erasures and scratched-out words may mean that you change your mind a lot or that your work is always sloppy. Follow the tips below and your filled-out form will work *for* you, instead of *against* you.

Words to Know

Marital status — are you single or married?

Prior work history — the jobs you've held before

References — people who know your character and your work

Relationship — is the person your parent, brother, cousin, etc.?

Tips on Filling Out Forms

● Read carefully before you start so that you can avoid erasures.
● Print or type, do not write in script or longhand, on a form. If you must print, use only one style — straight or slant. Do not mix styles. Your finished form will look much neater this way.

Milford High School   *Milford High School*
Straight   **Slant**

● Answer all questions and fill in all the blanks. If the question does not apply to you, write *N/A* on the blank. (*N/A* means "Not Applicable.")
● If the form provides answer boxes (❑), put a check (✔) in the box next to your answer.
● Spell all words correctly.
● Use up-to-date facts.
● If there are terms you do not understand, ask somebody for help. Better yet, look them up in the dictionary.

1. Print the alphabet in capital and small letters on the lines below. Remember to use only one style. All tall letters hould have the same height. Short letters should have the same size too.

Aa Bb Cc Dd Ee Ff Gg Hh Ii Jj Kk Ll Mm

Nn Oo Pp Qq Rr Ss Tt Uu Vv Ww Xx Yy Zz

2. Suppose you are applying for the job described in this ad. Fill out the application below.

POSITION APPLIED FOR				DATE	

NAME IN FULL	LAST	FIRST	MIDDLE	MAIDEN NAME	SOC. SEC. NO.

NUMBER AND STREET		CITY	STATE	ZIP	TELEPHONE NO.

MARITAL STATUS ☐ SINGLE ☐ MARRIED	PLACE OF BIRTH			DATE OF BIRTH

IN CASE OF EMERGENCY NOTIFY	NAME		RELATIONSHIP
	ADDRESS		TELEPHONE NO.

EDUCATION

TYPE OF SCHOOL	NAME AND ADDRESS	YRS. ATTENDED	YEAR LEFT	GRADUATED	COURSE OR MAJOR
GRAMMAR OR GRADE					
HIGH SCHOOL					
COLLEGE					
BUSINESS OR TRADE					

SKILLS

WHAT KIND OF WORK CAN YOU DO	TYPING SPEED
WHAT MACHINES CAN YOU OPERATE	SHORTHAND SPEED

PRIOR WORK HISTORY

LIST IN ORDER, LAST OR PRESENT EMPLOYER FIRST | MAY WE CALL YOUR PRESENT EMPLOYER ☐ YES ☐ NO

DATES FROM	TO	EMPLOYER	RATE OF PAY START FINISH	JOB TITLE AND SUPERVISOR'S NAME	REASON FOR LEAVING
		NAME			
		ADDRESS			
		NAME			
		ADDRESS			

REFERENCES (Other than Relatives or Former Employers)

NAME	ADDRESS	OCCUPATION
1.		
2.		

IT IS AGREED AND UNDERSTOOD THAT ANY FALSE STATEMENTS ON THIS APPLICATION MAY BE CONSIDERED SUFFICIENT CAUSE FOR DISMISSAL, WHEN DISCOVERED.

SIGNATURE_____

The Interview

Judging Relevance

The interview is your chance to persuade an employer to hire you instead of someone else. Good grooming and general appearance will help you make it through the door. But your ability to give answers that relate to the work will win the job for you.

Tips on Making a Good Impression

● Be sure you are neat and clean. Look as if you're ready to work.

● Be ready with your social security card, proof of age, or any working papers required in your state.

● Look interested and listen carefully to what the interviewer says.

● Remember, anything you say can be used *for* or *against* you. Answer the questions briefly and accurately. No matter how personal the question may sound, your answer must somehow relate to the job.

● Ask questions to show your sincere interest in the job: *What are the hours? What are my chances of learning on the job?*

Here is your chance to find out how well you can answer
questions at an interview.

1. Suppose you are being interviewed for the job
described in the ad at the right. And suppose that
all the answers listed under each question are true.
Which answer will you give? Put a check in the box next
to your answer.

a. What kind of work have you done before?

❏ I have collected records of the Bee Gees.
☑ I worked as a part-time salesperson at Casey's.
❏ I have been a baby-sitter, a dog-walker, and a basketball player.

b. Why are you interested in working for this store?

☑ I like records, especially selling them to people.
❏ I need a job, and you have an opening.
❏ All my friends come to this store, and I want to see them often.

2. Now you are being interviewed for a job as a
proofreader. Which answer will you give? Put a
check in the box next to your answer.

a. What makes you think you could do a good job?

❏ I have good ideas and I work fast.
☑ I pay attention to details and I can spot grammatical
errors quickly.
❏ I write good stories, especially when I'm given a lot of time.

b. How did you do in school?

❏ Terrible. I failed math because I didn't like the teacher.
❏ Fine, I guess.
☑ My average is C, but I got A's in English.

c. What do you hope to be, eventually?

❏ I hope to be a very rich person.
❏ I'd like to be the employer instead of the employee.
☑ I want to be somebody with a good job in publishing.

3. Think of three questions that you would like to ask
about the part-time job described in the ad. Write them
on the lines below.

a. _What are the part-time working hours?_
_____

b. _What kind of animals will I be working with?_
_____

c. _How much is the pay?_
_____

13

Vocabulary Review

1. See how many abbreviations you can figure out from the list under **Column A**. Choose the matching whole word from the list under **Column B**. On the line next to each abbreviation, write the letter for the correct word.

Column A		Column B	
appt	_d_	**a.**	full-time
ass't	_f_	**b.**	part-time
bkpr	_j_	**c.**	temporary
clk	_g_	**d.**	appointment
dept	_i_	**e.**	graduate
exp	_h_	**f.**	assistant
F/T	_a_	**g.**	clerk
grad	_e_	**h.**	experience
intvw	_o_	**i.**	department
mgr	_k_	**j.**	bookkeeper
opr	_n_	**k.**	manager
P/T	_b_	**l.**	secretary
pref'd	_m_	**m.**	preferred
sec	_l_	**n.**	operator
temp	_c_	**o.**	interview

2. Rewrite the following want ads, using whole words.

P/T clk, asst to bkpr. Exp pref'd. Call for appt. 555-2970

F/T tel opr. No exp nec. Call 555-2302

Part-time clerk,

assistant to bookkeeper.

Experience preferred.

Call for appointment.

555-2950

Full-time operator.

No experience necessary.

Call 555-2302

Reading Skills Review

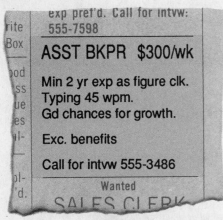

Job A

Job B

1. Carefully read the information in the ads at the left. See how they are alike and how they are different. Then answer the questions.

a. Which job pays more? ___Job A___

b. Which job requires less experience? ___Job B___

c. For which job would it be helpful to have neat and legible handwriting? ___Job B___

d. Which job promises that you can get ahead? ___Job A___

e. How do both jobs compare? How are they alike?

Both jobs promise excellent ___benefits___.

Both jobs require previous ___experience___.

Both jobs deal with ___bookkeeping___.

2. For which of the two jobs described in the ads at the left will each job applicant qualify?

a. Ann Jusko: "For the past three years, I've been working with numbers. I type 50 words per minute, I'm looking for a job that will let me move up." ___Job A___

b. Art Rosen: "I have to move to Florida and I need a clerical job. I can't type, but I can write neatly and legibly. I have been a figure clerk since last year." ___Job B___

Writing Skills Review

1. Practice filling out the W-4 form below. It is one of the forms you must fill out before you start on a job. It tells how much money should be withheld from your salary for taxes.

(Students' written information will vary.)

------------ Cut here and give the certificate to your employer. Keep the top portion for your records. ------------

| Form **W - 4**
Department of the Treasury
Internal Revenue Service | **Employee's Withholding Allowance Certificate**
▶**For Privacy Act and Paperwork Reduction Act Notice, see reverse.** | OMB No. 1545-0010
1989 |

| **1** Type or print your first name and middle initial | Last name | **2** Your social security number |

| Home address (number and street or rural route)

City or town, state, and ZIP code | **3** Marital
Status | ❑ Single ❑ Married
❑ Married, but withhold at higher Single rate.
Note: *If married, but legally separated, or spouse is a nonresident alien, check the Single box.* |

4 Total number of allowances you are claiming (from line G above or from the Worksheets on back if they apply) **4**

5 Additional amount, if any, you want deducted from each pay .... **5** $

6 I claim exemption from withholding and I certify that I meet **ALL** of the following conditions for exemption:
- Last year I had a right to a refund of **ALL** Federal income tax withheld because I had **NO** tax liability; **AND**
- This year I expect a refund of **ALL** Federal income tax withheld because I expect to have **NO** tax liability; **AND**
- This year if my income exceeds $500 and includes nonwage income, another person cannot claim me as a dependent.

If you meet all of the above conditions, enter the year effective and "EXEMPT" here .... ▶ **6** 19

7 Are you a full-time student? (Note: Full-time students are not automatically exempt.) .... **7** ❑ Yes ❑ No

Under penalties of perjury, I certify that I am entitled to the number of withholding allowances claimed on this certificate or entitled to claim exempt status.

Employee's signature ▶   Date ▶   , 19

| **8** Employer's name and address (**Employer:** Complete 8 and 10 **only if sending to IRS**) | **9** Office code (optional) | **10** Employer identification number |

---

2. Identify the parts of this business letter.

return address

date

inside address

greeting

body or content

closing

signature and name

> 2905 Woodlawn Drive
> Nashville, Tennessee 37215

> Februrary 6, 1990

> Mr. R. Woods
> Consumer Information Center
> Pueblo, Colorado 81009

> Dear Mr. Woods:

> I would like to order your publication number 021F entitled <u>Merchandising Your Job Talents</u>. I have enclosed a check in the amount of $2.00 as payment for one copy.

> Truly yours,

> *Lucille Stratton*
> Lucille Stratton

Unit 2

Working in Stores

If you would like to work in a store, your chances of getting a job will depend on your mastery of some basic skills — reading signs, price lists, and tax charts; categorizing items; following and giving directions; abbreviating; comparing labels; and filling out forms. This unit will enable you to learn and to apply these skills in specific jobs at different stores.

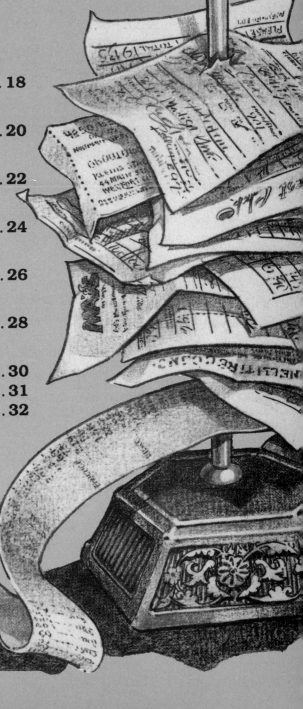

Stock Clerk

Reading Signs and Categorizing

Very few people know more than the stock clerk about the specific goods that are sold in a store. In fact, it's the stock clerk to whom most people turn when they can't seem to find the item they want. In addition to knowing how to read signs and labels, stock clerks have to be able to follow and give directions.

Tips

● Items in nearly all stores — from drugstores to hardware stores — are grouped in categories.

HAND TOOLS
- hammers
- small saws
- pliers
- wrenches

rakes
lawn mowers
tillers
lawn sprinklers

What do the items on the lower sign have in common?

● Items are stocked on shelves on either side of an aisle. A large store, such as a supermarket, will have several aisles.

● Each aisle has two sides — right and left. But right and left depend on which way you're facing. When you give directions to customers, make sure your "right" and their "right" are the same.

Words to Know

Category — a class or group

Stock — the goods sold in a store

A Frozen Foods, Dairy

1

B Deli, Meat

A Produce, Salad Dressing

2

B Baking Needs, Bread

A Noodles, Spaghetti, Tomato Sauce

3

B Snacks, Beverages, Tea, Coffee

A Canned Goods, Dietetic Foods

4

B Pickles, Condiments, Spices, Sugar

A Paper Goods, Pet Supplies

5

B Household Supplies, Cleansers

1. Study the supermarket aisles on the opposite page. You have to stock the shelves with each of the items listed. Where would you put them? Write the aisle locations on the lines provided. The first one is done for you.

Items to be stocked	Aisled location
a. cream cheese	1A
b. iced tea	3B
c. fresh tomatoes	2A
d. canned tomatoes	4A
e. frozen ravioli	1A
f. black pepper	4B
g. napkins	5A
h. bleach	5B
i. flea collars	5A
j. pie shells	2B or 1A

2. You work in a discount drugstore whose floor plan is shown at the right. Various customers have asked you where they can find certain items. The chart below shows your location at the time and the items the customers are looking for. What directions would you give them? Fill in the chart with the correct aisle number and the correct side of the aisle. The first one has been done for you.

Rear of store

DISCOUNT DRUGS Rx

Cosmetics | 1 | Pain Relievers | First-Aid Supplies | 2 | Foot Care | Deodorant | 3 | Cold Remedies | Dental Needs | 4 | Hair Products | Shaving Needs | 5 | Baby Needs | Skin Care | 6 | Prescriptions

Your location	Product requested	Aisle	Side
aisle 3, front	razor blades	5	Left
aisle 6, front	bandages	2	Left
aisle 2, rear	cough medicine	3	Left
aisle 1, front	shampoo	4	Right
aisle 1, rear	hand cream	6	Right
aisle 4, front	diapers	5	Right

Bakery Sales Clerk

Reading Price List

A bakery is a great place to work. Where else can you be surrounded by the aroma or smell of freshly baked goods and earn money at the same time? Like most stores, the bakery lists its prices on a menu board behind the counter. This makes your job easier.

Sometimes goods are sold in more than one size.

Run your eyes across the chart until you find the correct price.

This is the specific item.

Find the correct category of the items.

BREADS — ROLLS

	SM	LG
White	.65	.95
Rye	.85	1.25
Bran	.95	1.05
Salt free		.90
Hard rolls		2/.75
Soft rolls		.35

CAKES

Layer	$7.50
Angel	7.00
Pound	6.00
Chocolate	9.50
Carrot	7.00

PIES

	6"	8"	10"
Fruit	$5.25	$7.25	$9.50
Lemon chiffon			15.00
Pumpkin	5.25	7.75	9.95
Custard	7.75		
Cheese	8.00		

Freezer & Refrigerator

Ice cream roll	$5.95
Rum cake	8.50
Boston cream	9.00
Fruit flair	14.00
Ice cream cakes 10"	14.50
14"	16.00

COFFEE CAKES

Rings	$2.00
Pecan	3.00
Crumb	2.00
Apple	2.25

COOKIES

Large	.90
Small	$6.25/lb.

PASTRIES

Danish	.90
Turnovers	.90
Cupcakes	.85
Fruit tarts	.80
Eclairs	.80
Donuts	.55

Baked goods are generally sold:

- singly
- as a cost-saving special by twos
- as an additional cost-saving special by the dozen
- by the pound (usually for cookies and small pastries)

1.

Refer to the price list on the opposite page to answer the following questions.

a. How much is an eclair? _____ *80¢*

b. How much is an eight-inch cherry pie? _____ *$7.25*

c. How much is a large loaf of rye bread? _____ *$1.25*

d. Which is more expensive: an eight-inch fruit pie or an eight-inch pumpkin pie? _____ *pumpkin pie*

e. Which is more expensive: two donuts or two cupcakes?
_____ *two cupcakes*

f. How many pastries cost less than $.85? _____ *three*

g. How many items cost more than $9.50? _____ *five*

h. What is the most expensive item? _____ *14" ice cream cake*

i. What is the least expensive bread? _____ *soft roll*

2.

A customer comes into a bakery with a large order for a party. List the price opposite each item.

1	large loaf of rye bread	*$1.25*
1	small loaf of bran bread	*$ .95*
1	six-inch blueberry pie	*$5.25*
4	eclairs	*$3.20*

3.

A woman customer enters the store and wants four different desserts. She does not want to spend more than $3.50 on each item. She does not want anything that has fruit or cheese in it. List eight suggestions for her.

Answers will vary, but bread should

not be included and each item should

not cost more than $3.50.

_____

_____

_____

_____

_____

Cashier

Reading a Sales Tax Chart

Part of your job as a cashier is figuring out the right amount of sales tax to charge your customer. A sales tax is the amount of money that goes to the government. The sales tax amount depends on the amount of the sale. A Sales Tax Chart helps cashiers to figure out the tax for each sale.

Words to Know

Taxable item — something that is taxed when purchased

Range — the amounts that have the same sales tax

Tips

For Reading a Tax Chart

● Move your eyes down the **Amount of Sale** column until you find the correct price range.

Sale $7.98

What is the price range of an item costing $7.98? _7.93–8.07_

● Once you have found the correct range, move your eyes across to the **Tax to be Collected** column. The amount you see is the sales tax. Add this amount to the original purchase price to get the total price.

What is the total price for an item costing $3.15? ___3.37___

ST-110.7

7% SALES AND USE TAX COLLECTION CHART 7%

The current tax rate

The chart has two columns. What are they?

Amount of Sale	Tax to be Collected	Amount of Sale	Tax to be Collected
$0.01 to $0.10	None	$5.08 to $5.21	$.36
.11 to .20	1¢	5.22 to 5.35	.37
.21 to .33	2¢	5.36 to 5.49	.38
.34 to .47	3¢	5.50 to 5.64	.39
.48 to .62	4¢	5.65 to 5.78	.40
.63 to .76	5¢	5.79 to 5.92	.41
.77 to .91	6¢	5.93 to 6.07	.42
.92 to 1.07	7¢	6.08 to 6.21	.43
1.08 to 1.21	8¢	6.22 to 6.35	.44
1.22 to 1.35	9¢	6.36 to 6.49	.45
1.36 to 1.49	$.10	6.50 to 6.64	.46
1.50 to 1.64	.11	6.65 to 6.78	.47
1.65 to 1.78	.12	6.79 to 6.92	.48
1.79 to 1.92	.13	6.93 to 7.07	.49
1.93 to 2.07	.14	7.08 to 7.21	.50
2.08 to 2.21	.15	7.22 to 7.35	.51
2.22 to 2.35	.16	7.36 to 7.49	.52
2.36 to 2.49	.17	7.50 to 7.64	.53
2.50 to 2.64	.18	7.65 to 7.78	.54
2.65 to 2.78	.19	7.79 to 7.92	.55
2.79 to 2.92	.20	7.93 to 8.07	.56
2.93 to 3.07	.21	8.08 to 8.21	.57
3.08 to 3.21	.22	8.22 to 8.35	.58
3.22 to 3.35	.23	8.36 to 8.49	.59
3.36 to 3.49	.24	8.50 to 8.64	.60
3.50 to 3.64	.25	8.65 to 8.78	.61
3.65 to 3.78	.26	8.79 to 8.92	.62
3.79 to 3.92	.27	8.93 to 9.07	.63
3.93 to 4.07	.28	9.08 to 9.21	.64
4.08 to 4.21	.29	9.22 to 9.35	.65
4.22 to 4.35	.30	9.36 to 9.49	.66
4.36 to 4.49	.31	9.50 to 9.64	.67
4.50 to 4.64	.32	9.65 to 9.78	.68
4.65 to 4.78	.33	9.79 to 9.92	.69
4.79 to 4.92	.34	9.93 to 10.00	.70
4.93 to 5.07	.35		

On sales over $10.00, compute the tax by multiplying the amount of sale by the applicable tax rate and rounding the result to the nearest whole cent.

The Amount of Sale column lists price ranges.

The chart lists the tax on items costing up to 10 dollars. What should you do to figure out the tax on items over 10 dollars?

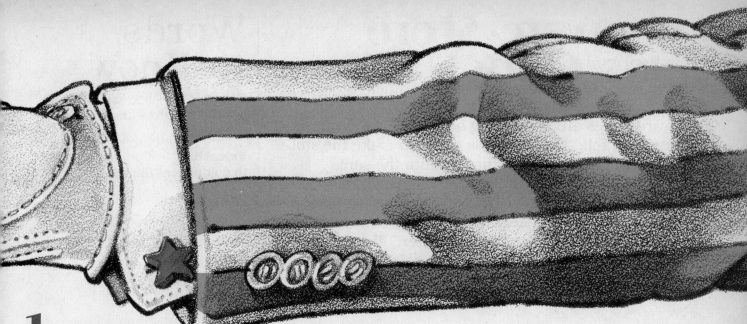

1. Using the Sales Tax Chart on the opposite page, find the correct sales price range for each of the following purchase prices.

a. $2.49   _2.36 – 2.49_

b. $3.08   _3.08 – 3.21_

c. $1.15   _1.08 – 1.21_

d. $7.38   _7.36 – 7.49_

e. $5.20   _5.08 – 5.21_

f. $9.19   _9.08 – 9.21_

g. $4.89   _4.79 – 4.92_

h. $7.32   _7.22 – 7.35_

i. $6.08   _6.08 – 6.21_

j. $0.59   _0.48 – 0.62_

2. Using the Sales Tax Chart, find the correct tax on each of the following items.

a. 1 six-pack of soda — $3.29   _.23_

b. 1 box of tissues — $0.90   _.06_

c. 1 hardcover book — $9.95   _.70_

d. 1 photograph album — $8.95   _.63_

e. 1 roll of film — $5.39   _.38_

f. 1 pen — $4.98   _.35_

g. 1 nylon knapsack — $9.98   _.70_

h. 1 T-shirt — $7.99   _.56_

3. Using the Sales Tax Chart, circle the prices in each group that have the same sales tax.

a.	(.38)	(.37)	.33	(.42)	.48
b.	(2/1.95)	(2.05)	(3/2.00)	2.10	1.89
c.	(8.50)	(8.60)	8.70	8.65	8.45
d.	5.19	(5.25)	5.54	(5.35)	(5.30)
e.	4.17	(3/4.00)	(3.98/doz.)	4.25	3.90

23

Hardware Store Sales Clerk

Reading and Comparing Labels

Hardware stores are fascinating because of the hundreds of items they sell. However, this can also make the store very confusing. Even items that fall into the same category — paint, for example — vary somewhat depending on the requirements of the job. A big part of your job as a hardware store sales clerk is to be able to explain these differences to the customer. This means reading and understanding product labels.

The Basics

When a customer asks for an item to do a particular job, he or she is first interested in the basics:

- **size, quantity, or capacity**
- **suitability** — what is the product used for?

TUF-HOLD CEMENT

For: china, glass, metal, leather, wood, paper

1½ fl. oz. .052 liter

suitability   *size, quantity, or capacity*

Would you recommend this product for plastic?   *No*

The Particulars

The customer may also be concerned with:

 ease of application or use — is it simple or easy to use?
 versatility — how many ways can a product be used?

STAY BRIGHT CAR WAX

★ Cleans ★ Prevents Rust
★ Shines ★ Protects Paint

DIRECTIONS: Spray a thin coat of STAY BRITE and rub in circular strokes with a dry cloth.

Compare directions or instructions.

Which brand requires less work?

Which brand does more?

MIRROR CAR WAX

Protects your car's finish while it shines

Directions
Apply a thin coat with a damp cloth or sponge. When the wax dries to a white film, buff with a dry cloth.

1. A customer knows very little about fertilizer, and he has a lot of questions. Answer each of his questions by writing the name of the right fertilizer on the line provided.

a. Which fertilizer is suitable for tulip bulbs? _____All-Grow_____

b. Which fertilizer does not have to be mixed with water? _____Maxi Flor_____

c. Which fruit tree fertilizer is the easiest to use? _____Maxi Flor_____

d. Which fertilizer has to be applied twice a year? _____Green Thumb_____

e. Which one would you recommend for a vegetable garden that measures 40 sq. ft.? _____All-Grow (2 bags)_____

f. Which one can be used in the greatest number of situations? _____All-Grow_____

g. Which fertilizer is suitable for flowers? _____All-Grow_____

h. Which one cannot be applied in September? _____All Grow_____

2. On the line provided, write the name of the fertilizer you would recommend to each of the following customers.

a. Mrs. Gatsby wants a fertilizer for the bushes that border the front of her house. It is August, and she wants to apply the fertilizer immediately. _____Maxi Flor_____

b. Mr. Stephens wants to fertilize his lawn, but he does not want to spend more money than is absolutely necessary. _____Green Thumb_____

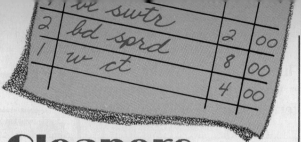

	bl swtr		
2	bd sprd	2	00
1	w ct	8	00
		4	00

At the Cleaners

Using Abbreviations to Fill Out a Ticket

Filling out a dry-cleaning store ticket is like writing a secret message. There's a lot of information to put on the ticket. But everything has to be in codes — in abbreviated form — to save time and space. If you take some time to learn how to abbreviate, you too can write secret codes at the cleaners.

Tips

for Abbreviating

● Abbreviations are short, usually no more than four letters.

dress = dr
skirt = skt
blanket = blkt

● Most abbreviations have no vowels.

jacket = jkt
sweater = swtr

● Abbreviations for words that begin with the same two or three letters should be different.

blue = bl
black = blk
green = gr
gray = gry

To Fill Out a Dry-Cleaning Ticket

Use the standard abbreviated form for dates: month/day/year.

The customer's name should not be abbreviated. Do you know why?

What parts of the customer's address can be abbreviated?

DATE 4/17/80

Store hours: M-F 7am to 7pm · Sat. 7am to 5 pm

VALU CLEANERS
15 Miller St. Wichita, Kansas

NAME Eloise Nelson

ADDRESS 3 Willow Rd.

QTY.	ITEM	PRICE	
		3	75
1	bl skt	3	75
1	r skt	4	—
1	gr swtr		
		11	50

MON TUE WED (THURS) FRI SAT

Indicate the cost of each item. Add the prices and write the total.

Circle the day the items will be ready.

26

1. Write the abbreviations for these items on the blanks provided below.

Price Chart

Blankets	Drapes	Coats	Tablecloths	Jackets
$6.00	$15.00	$7.00	$4.50	$5.00

Dresses	Sweaters	Skirts	Slacks	Suits
$4.95	$4.00	$3.75	$4.75	$9.95

embr pld gr
cvr ct cl
y skt sl bl
str
r dr drp
wh bd sprd
jkt
tbl cl br gd
bg

a. green drapes ____*gr drp*____

b. yellow plaid skirt ____*y pld skt*____

c. beige jacket ____*bg jkt*____

d. striped bedspread ____*str bd sprd*____

e. brown slacks ____*br sl*____

f. red striped dress ____*r str dr*____

g. white tablecloth ____*wh tbl cl*____

h. blue plaid coat ____*bl pld ct*____

2. Fill out the dry-cleaning tickets below for each customer. Put today's date on the tickets and indicate that the articles will be ready in one week. Refer to the price chart for the cost of each item.

a. Michael De Rosa, who lives at 325 Eighth Avenue, brought in a brown coat, a pair of green plaid slacks, two blue jackets, a beige sweater, and a red blanket.

b. Lily Chan of 935 Chestnut Street brought in a black skirt, a pair of blue drapes, a striped tablecloth, and a gold dress.

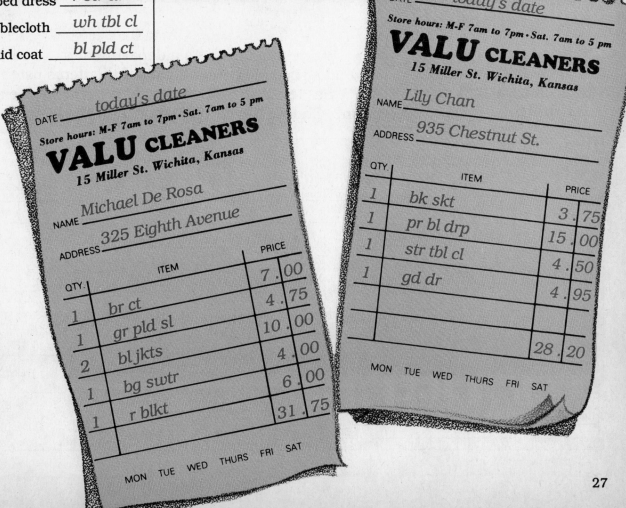

DATE __today's date__

Store hours: M-F 7am to 7pm · Sat. 7am to 5 pm

VALU CLEANERS
15 Miller St. Wichita, Kansas

NAME __Michael De Rosa__

ADDRESS __325 Eighth Avenue__

QTY.	ITEM	PRICE	
		7	00
1	br ct	4	75
1	gr pld sl	10	00
2	bl jkts	4	00
1	bg swtr	6	00
1	r blkt	31	75

MON   TUE   WED   THURS   FRI   SAT

DATE __today's date__

Store hours: M-F 7am to 7pm · Sat. 7am to 5 pm

VALU CLEANERS
15 Miller St. Wichita, Kansas

NAME __Lily Chan__

ADDRESS __935 Chestnut St.__

QTY.	ITEM	PRICE	
1	bk skt	3	75
1	pr bl drp	15	00
1	str tbl cl	4	50
1	gd dr	4	95
		28	20

MON   TUE   WED   THURS   FRI   SAT

Words to Know

Cardholder — the person to whom the credit card is issued

Expired — came to an end

Sales draft — the form on which the credit card sale is written up

Subtotal — the amount before the tax or other charges are added

Valid — legal for use

The Salesperson Takes the Credit

Using Credit Card Forms

Over the past few years, credit cards have become so common that the customer is often tempted to ask, "Do you accept cash?" Department store salespeople have to familiarize themselves with credit card forms in order to accommodate the tens of thousands of people who say, "Charge it!"

The Credit Card

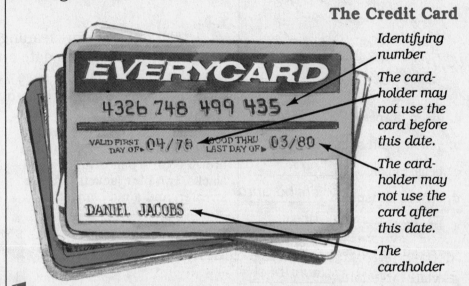

Identifying number

The cardholder may not use the card before this date.

The cardholder may not use the card after this date.

The cardholder

1. Study this form. As a department store salesperson, you must be able to identify all of the items listed on page 29. What letter should you write in each blank circle on the form? Choose the correct letter from the list on page 29.

The Credit Card Sales Draft

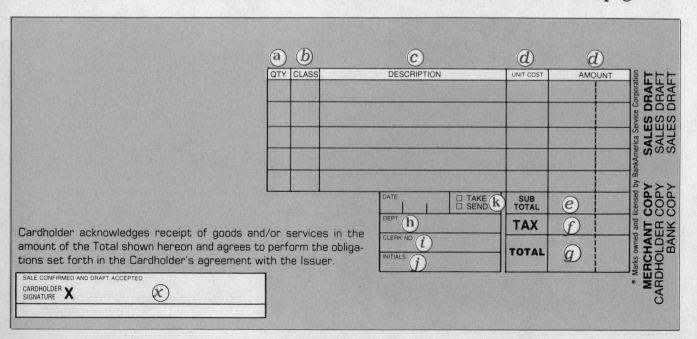

Cardholder acknowledges receipt of goods and/or services in the amount of the Total shown hereon and agrees to perform the obligations set forth in the Cardholder's agreement with the Issuer.

a. The quantity. How many of each item were purchased?

b. The class. Department stores classify items according to number. This is an instant identification.

c. Description. Very briefly, describe the item purchased. Use abbreviations.

d. Unit cost and amount. The unit cost is the cost of *one* item. The total amount depends on how many of the particular items the customer purchased. Multiply the *quantity* by the *unit cost.*

e. Subtotal. The total cost of the items purchased before the tax is added

f. Tax. The amount of tax based on the subtotal

g. Total. The subtotal plus the tax

h. Department number. Every department in a large store is numbered (for example: shoes — 31: toys — 18: ladies' wear — 52).

i. The clerk's number. That's you, if you're the salesperson. Like the departments, you are also identified by a number.

j. Initials. Write your initials to verify your sale.

k. Take/Send. Is the customer taking the item or will it be delivered to the customer's house?

l. Cardholder's signature. Check this against the signature on the back of the credit card to make sure they match. Never ask the customer to sign the sales draft until you have written in the total cost of the purchase.

2. You work for Alpine Sports, a large sporting goods department store. You are clerk number 28. Today you are in Department 33 — ski equipment. Daniel Jacobs used his credit card to pay for a pair of $93 ski boots, a set of $22 ski poles, and three pairs of thermal socks at $2.50 a pair. The tax is $8.58. The customer will take his purchases with him. Use the credit card form below to write up the sale.

QTY	CLASS	DESCRIPTION	UNIT COST	AMOUNT	
1		pair of ski boots	$ 93	93	00
1		set of ski poles	22	22	00
3		pairs of thermal sock	2.50	7	50

DATE *today's date* ☑ TAKE ☐ SEND — SUB TOTAL 122 50

DEPT. *33* — TAX 8 58

CLERK NO. *28*

INITIALS *student's initial* — TOTAL 131 08

Cardholder acknowledges receipt of goods and/or services in the amount of the Total shown hereon and agrees to perform the obligations set forth in the Cardholder's agreement with the Issuer.

SALE CONFIRMED AND DRAFT ACCEPTED
CARDHOLDER SIGNATURE **X**

® Marks owned and licensed by BankAmerica Service Corporation

SALES DRAFT SALES DRAFT SALES DRAFT

MERCHANT COPY CARDHOLDER COPY BANK COPY

Vocabulary Review

1. Hidden among the letters of this puzzle are some of the words you learned in this unit. Can you find them? Hint: Look left to right, top to bottom, and diagonally.

D	C	A	T	E	G	O	R	Y	S
T	A	S	P	K	Z	M	A	Q	R
P	R	I	U	Z	D	F	N	E	T
C	D	G	H	B	W	X	G	J	K
Z	H	D	R	J	T	K	E	M	O
U	O	B	T	S	T	O	C	K	N
E	L	F	G	T	A	R	T	S	M
H	D	E	C	L	A	I	R	A	L
I	E	X	P	I	R	E	D	X	L
J	R	K	L	C	L	A	I	M	F

2. Use the words you found to complete the sentences at the right.

a. Green beans, tomatoes, and carrots may be grouped under the same ___category___.

b. The person to whom a credit card is issued is the ___cardholder___.

c. The lowest and highest amounts that have the same sales tax make up the ___price range___ for that tax.

d. The ___net___ weight of a package does not include the packaging.

e. The sum of purchases before tax is added is called the ___subtotal___.

f. When goods for sale arrive in a store, they are put in ___stock___.

g. You can find the price of fruit ___tarts___ under "Pastries."

h. An oblong cream puff is called an ___eclair___.

i. Before accepting a credit card, be sure that its validity has not ___expired___.

j. To get your clothes back from the cleaners, you must present your ___claim___ ticket.

Reading Skills Review

1. Read this supermarket sign and answer the questions.

a. You are directly in front of the sign when the customer asks you where the carrots are. Should you point to the left or to the right?

left

b. On which side should iced tea be stocked?

right

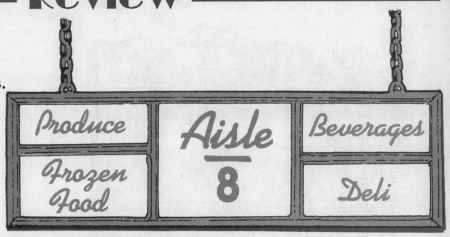

2. Use the chart on the right to find the price of each item described below.

a. 9 oz. bean sprouts at 70¢ per lb. ___.39___

b. 1/2 lb. grapes at 69¢ per lb. ___.35___

c. 1/4 lb. beans at 67¢ per lb. ___.17___

	Price per Pound					
Weight	$.65	$.66	$.67	$.68	$.69	$.70
1 oz.	.04	.04	.04	.04	.04	.04
2 oz.	.08	.08	.08	.09	.09	.09
3 oz.	.12	.12	.13	.13	.13	.13
4 oz.	.16	.17	.17	.17	.17	.18
5 oz.	.20	.21	.21	.21	.22	.22
6 oz.	.24	.25	.25	.26	.26	.26
7 oz.	.28	.29	.29	.30	.30	.31
8 oz.	.33	.33	.34	.34	.35	.35
9 oz.	.37	.37	.38	.38	.39	.39
10 oz.	.41	.41	.42	.43	.43	.44
11 oz.	.45	.45	.46	.47	.47	.48
12 oz.	.49	.50	.50	.51	.52	.53
13 oz.	.53	.54	.54	.55	.56	.57
14 oz.	.57	.58	.59	.60	.60	.61
15 oz.	.61	.62	.63	.64	.65	.66
1 lb.	.65	.66	.67	.68	.69	.70

3. Read the labels on the right. Which product would you recommend for each customer described below? Write the product's name on the line provided.

a. Cristina's car has a few rusty spots. Which polish does she need?

Miracle Polish

b. Larry wants to polish his car without working too hard. Which polish should he use?

Perfect Car Polish

31

Writing Skills
Review

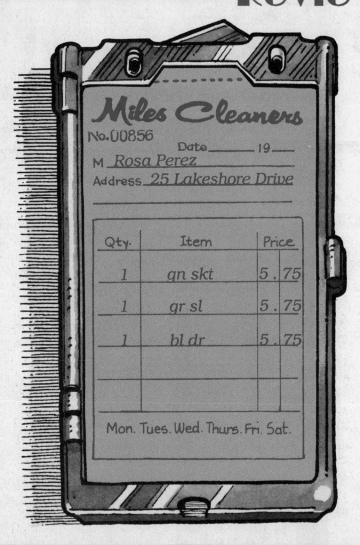

Miles Cleaners

No. 00856

Date_____ 19____

M _Rosa Perez_

Address _25 Lakeshore Drive_

Qty.	Item	Price
1	gn skt	5 . 75
1	gr sl	5 . 75
1	bl dr	5 . 75

Mon. Tues. Wed. Thurs. Fri. Sat.

1. Fill out this dry-cleaning ticket for Rosa Perez, who lives at 25 Lakeshore Drive. She has a green skirt, a pair of gray slacks, and a blue dress. The price for cleaning each item is $5.75. Put today's date on the ticket, and indicate that the articles will be ready in one week.

2. Suppose you work in Spare Time, a big hobby store that accepts credit cards. You are clerk number 45 and you are in department 20. Angela Lu buys the following items:

One model spaceship kit — $9.95

One tube of model kit glue — $1.29

Five small jars of paint — $1.10 each

One paintbrush — $.89

The tax is $1.41. Ms. Lu wants the items sent to her home. Use the credit card form at the left to write up the sale.

QTY	CLASS	DESCRIPTION	UNIT COST	AMOUNT	
1		mdl spshp kt	9.95	9	95
1		tb mdl kt gl	1.29	1	29
5		jr pnt	1.10	5	50
1		pnt br	.89		89

DATE	☐ TAKE ☐ SEND	SUB TOTAL	17	63
DEPT. 20		TAX	1	41
CLERK NO. 45				
INITIALS student's init.		TOTAL	19	04

of goods and/or services in the and agrees to perform the obliga- agreement with the Issuer.

® Marks owned and licensed by BankAmerica Service Corporation

SALES DRAFT SALES DRAFT SALES DRAFT

MERCHANT COPY CARDHOLDER COPY BANK COPY

Unit 3

General Office Work

Skills such as alphabetizing, categorizing, reading maps and directories, sorting mail, and taking messages are useful in many different job situations. Apply these skills as you work in the following office jobs.

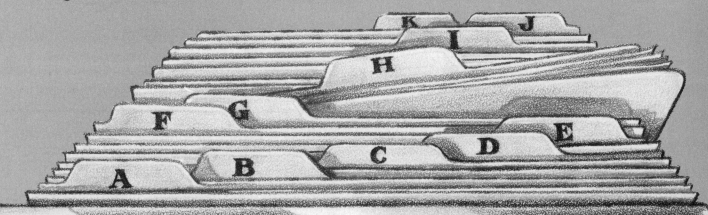

The File Clerk

Alphabetizing

A dictionary is easy to use because all the words are shown in alphabetical order. Company records must also be kept on file alphabetically so they can be found easily when needed. Your job as a file clerk is to establish and maintain the order. To start, all you need to know is the alphabet.

Tips

for Alphabetizing

● People's names are alphabetized by last name.

● When two last names are spelled the same, alphabetize by first name.

● When two words or names begin with the same letter, alphabetize according to the second letter. If the first two letters are the same, alphabetize according to the third letter.

Delano, Edith
Franz, Herbert
Greenspan, Arlene

Lindsey, Carol
Ludlow, Jeffrey

Travers, John
Travers, Louis
Travers, Sandra

Holt, Raymond
Hopper, Grace

Special Situations

● When the articles *the*, *an*, or *a* are part of a title or company name, the articles are not considered when alphabetizing. Alphabetize according to the first word after the article.

● When letters or initials are part of the company name, alphabetize according to the first letter.

● When numbers are part of the company name, alphabetize according to the spelling of the number.

The Heath Corporation
The Miller Company

this

C. F. Bowes, Inc
D. Ames Company

not this

Four

4-Leaf Clover Company
100 Candles, Inc.

One hundred

1. You work for a law firm and are asked to alphabetize the files on the following clients. On the lines provided, write the number *1* next to the client who would come first alphabetically; *2* next to the client who would come second alphabetically; and so on.

- __2__ Albert Gibbs
- __9__ The Maxwell Company
- __5__ Adolph Mason
- __1__ Louise Baker-Pearson
- __10__ Dennis McMannis
- __6__ Elvira Massey
- __7__ Jeffrey Masson
- __3__ The Gibson Corporation
- __12__ 1-2-3 Flooring, Inc.
- __8__ Arlette Maxwell
- __4__ Kathleen MacNamara
- __11__ Phillip Odette

2. Alphabetize the following files on the blanks provided.

Price Lists
Clients, Eastern Region
Sales Reports
Products, Descriptions
Memorandums
Status Reports
Sales Brochures
Sales Forms
Clients, Western Region
Mailing Lists
Sales Contracts
Budget Reports
Products, Proposed
Sales Meeting Reports

Budget Reports

Clients, Eastern Region

Clients, Western Region

Mailing Lists

Memorandums

Price Lists

Products, Descriptions

Products, Proposed

Sales Brochures

Sales Contracts

Sales Forms

Sales Meeting Reports

Sales Reports

Status Reports

File Clerk

Categorizing

When a company grows, its filing system becomes more elaborate. Documents and letters can no longer be filed alphabetically in folders that read A, B, C, and so forth. So, as the file clerk, you find that you have to establish categories.

Words to Know

Category — a class or group of items

Chronologically — by the order in which things happen

Memorandum — a note or reminder usually sent to someone in the same office

Tips for Filing by Category

- There are two ways of quickly knowing the category of the item to be filed.

A. Does the item have a standard format, such as a bill, a letter, or a memorandum?
B. Does the item say what it's about?

- If the item cannot be identified through either of these two methods, scan the material to find out what it is about. Then decide which category it falls into.

MEMORANDUM —A

From: L. Stokes
To: All Sales Personnel
Date: 7/15/82
Subject: New Product Line —B

- Generally, there is a labeled folder for each category. The folders are filed alphabetically behind the alphabet dividers.

- Dated material in each category is filed chronologically. The most recent is filed first.

FAMILIARIZE YOURSELF WITH THE CATEGORIES IN THE FILE CABINET

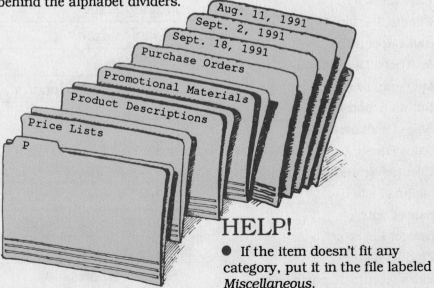

Aug. 11, 1991
Sept. 2, 1991
Sept. 18, 1991
Purchase Orders
Promotional Materials
Product Descriptions
Price Lists
P

HELP!

- If the item doesn't fit any category, put it in the file labeled *Miscellaneous.*

Apply your categorizing skills in the following situations:

1. Check the word or phrase that correctly completes each sentence.

a. A file labeled *Expense Reports* could contain

✔ records of employee expenses.

_____ petty cash forms, budgets, payment requests.

_____ checks, operating expenses.

b. A file containing letters to and from customers should be labeled

_____ *Mail, Outgoing.*

✔ *Correspondence.*

_____ *Contracts.*

c. The addresses of mail-order customers can be found in the file labeled

_____ *Records.*

_____ *Mail-Order Forms.*

✔ *Mailing List.*

d. You work for an insurance company. The Ribilow family has just taken out a policy on their new camper. You would file the forms on their new policy under

✔ *Clients — Ribilow.*

_____ *Policies.*

_____ *Policy Forms, New.*

e. A record of bills sent to clients would be found under

✔ *Billing.*

_____ *Clients.*

_____ *Records.*

2. You work in the front office of a high school and have been asked to locate all the items listed below. Write the category under which the item would be filed.

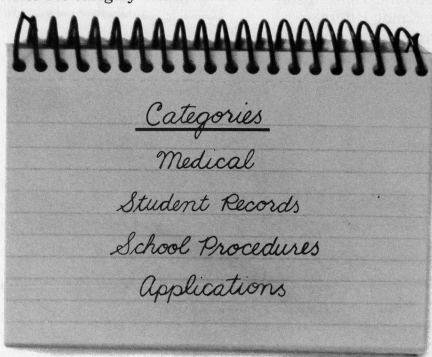

Categories

Medical

Student Records

School Procedures

Applications

a. fire drill procedure
School Procedures

b. health report
Medical

c. record card for Hector Reyes, a student
Student Records

d. Mrs. Taurin's job application
Applications

e. information sheet about what to do on field trips
School Procedures

3. You must file letters whose dates are shown below. Number the letters to show the order in which they should be filed.

_5_ December 12, 1988

_6_ 11/15/87

_4_ Feb. 6, 1989

_1_ May 20, 1990

_3_ 4/10/89

_2_ Mar. 3, '90

Mailroom Clerk

Sorting Mail

Large companies receive an enormous amount of mail daily. It is the job of the mailroom clerk to sort all incoming letters and parcels and then distribute them to the right person as quickly and efficiently as possible.

Words to Know

Addressee — the person to whom a letter or other correspondence is addressed

Incoming — coming in; arriving at (a company)

Parcel — a package, as opposed to a letter

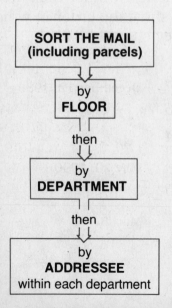

```
SORT THE MAIL
(including parcels)
       |
       v
      by
    FLOOR
       |
     then
       |
       v
      by
  DEPARTMENT
       |
     then
       |
       v
      by
  ADDRESSEE
within each department
```

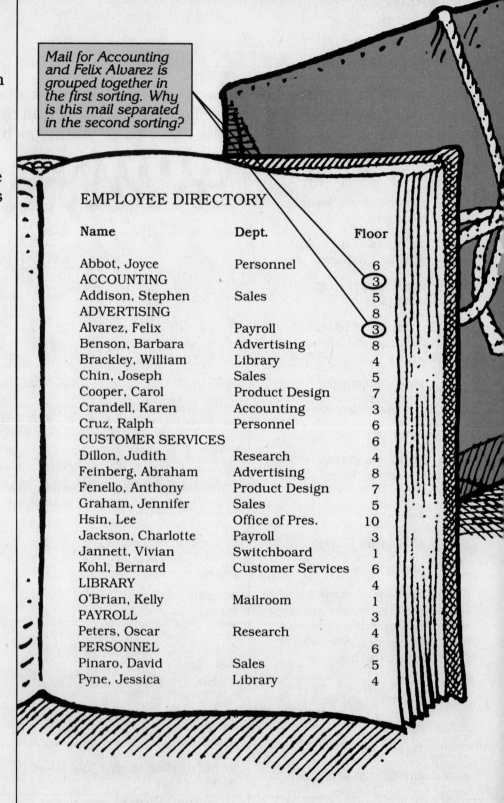

Mail for Accounting and Felix Alvarez is grouped together in the first sorting. Why is this mail separated in the second sorting?

EMPLOYEE DIRECTORY

Name	Dept.	Floor
Abbot, Joyce	Personnel	6
ACCOUNTING		3
Addison, Stephen	Sales	5
ADVERTISING		8
Alvarez, Felix	Payroll	3
Benson, Barbara	Advertising	8
Brackley, William	Library	4
Chin, Joseph	Sales	5
Cooper, Carol	Product Design	7
Crandell, Karen	Accounting	3
Cruz, Ralph	Personnel	6
CUSTOMER SERVICES		6
Dillon, Judith	Research	4
Feinberg, Abraham	Advertising	8
Fenello, Anthony	Product Design	7
Graham, Jennifer	Sales	5
Hsin, Lee	Office of Pres.	10
Jackson, Charlotte	Payroll	3
Jannett, Vivian	Switchboard	1
Kohl, Bernard	Customer Services	6
LIBRARY		4
O'Brian, Kelly	Mailroom	1
PAYROLL		3
Peters, Oscar	Research	4
PERSONNEL		6
Pinaro, David	Sales	5
Pyne, Jessica	Library	4

38

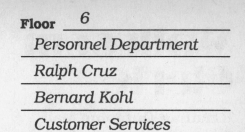

Refer to the employee directory on the opposite page to answer the questions that follow.

Floor ___6___

Personnel Department

Ralph Cruz

Bernard Kohl

Customer Services

Floor ___4___

William Brackley

Judith Dillon

Research Department

Floor ___3___

Felix Alvarez

Karen Crandell

Floor ___5___

Jennifer Graham

David Pinaro

Floor ___10___

Lee Hsin

1. You have to sort the mail addressed to the following people or departments by floor. First fill in the floor number. On the given lines, group the names by floor.

Felix Alvarez

Jennifer Graham

David Pinaro

Personnel Department

Ralph Cruz

William Brackley

Bernard Kohl

Customer Services

Lee Hsin

Judith Dillon

Research Department

Karen Crandell

Departmental mail that is not addressed to a particular person is delivered to the receptionist of that department.

2. The groups below represent piles of letters that have been sorted by floor and department. One letter in each group is in the wrong pile. Circle the name of the addressee on the missorted letter.

(Oscar Peters)
David Pinaro
Jennifer Graham
Stephen Addison

Personnel
Ralph Cruz
(Customer Services)
Joyce Abbot

Charlotte Jackson
Payroll
(Karen Crandell)
Felix Alvarez

Jessica Pyne
William Brackley
(Judith Dillon)
Library

3. The following parcels are going to different addresses in the Sales Department. Alphabetize the mail to make delivery faster and easier. Number the parcels in order from 1 to 4.

___4___ David Pinaro

___1___ Stephen Addison

___3___ Jennifer Graham

___2___ Joseph Chin

Mailroom Clerk

Handling Outgoing Mail

The mailroom clerk does a great deal more than just distribute company mail. There is also the business of outgoing mail — letters and packages that are sent from the company. Collection is easy — it's done floor by floor. But once the mail is in the mailroom, it must be sorted and inspected before the Post Office can take over.

Tips for Handling Outgoing Mail

Sorting

Letters	
local and state	out of state

Parcels	
local and state	out of state

Inspection

Mail can be handled more efficiently by the Post Office if it is first inspected for:

- packaging (how well a parcel is wrapped)
- correct state abbreviation
- zip codes

About the Zip Code Directory

States are listed in alphabetical order.

Cities and towns within each state are also listed in alphabetical order.

Large cities that have several zip codes are broken down into individual postal districts. These districts appear alphabetically in the appendix which follows the state's listing.

Among the listings in the appendix are Post Office branches and boxes, major buildings, named streets, numbered streets, and universities.

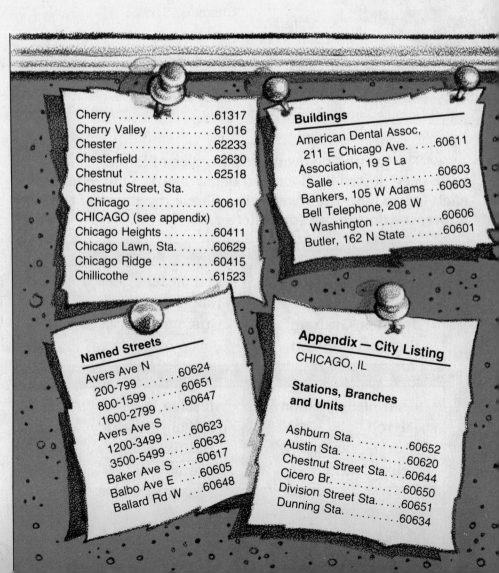

Cherry 61317
Cherry Valley 61016
Chester 62233
Chesterfield 62630
Chestnut 62518
Chestnut Street, Sta.
   Chicago 60610
CHICAGO (see appendix)
Chicago Heights 60411
Chicago Lawn, Sta. 60629
Chicago Ridge 60415
Chillicothe 61523

Buildings

American Dental Assoc,
  211 E Chicago Ave. 60611
Association, 19 S La
  Salle 60603
Bankers, 105 W Adams . .60603
Bell Telephone, 208 W
  Washington 60606
Butler, 162 N State 60601

Named Streets

Avers Ave N
  200-799 60624
  800-1599 60651
  1600-2799 60647
Avers Ave S
  1200-3499 60623
  3500-5499 60632
Baker Ave S 60617
Balbo Ave E 60605
Ballard Rd W . .60648

Appendix — City Listing

CHICAGO, IL

Stations, Branches and Units

Ashburn Sta. 60652
Austin Sta. 60620
Chestnut Street Sta. . . .60644
Cicero Br. 60650
Division Street Sta. 60651
Dunning Sta. 60634

1. Suppose the company you work for is in Manchester, Vermont. In which bin should each mail item go? Put a check mark in the correct bin.

a. letter to Washington, D.C.
b. package to San Francisco, California
c. letter to Manchester, Vermont
d. carton to Stowe, Vermont
e. birthday card to Kansas City
f. book bag to Bennington, Vermont
g. letter to Austin, Texas
h. letter to Rutland, Vermont

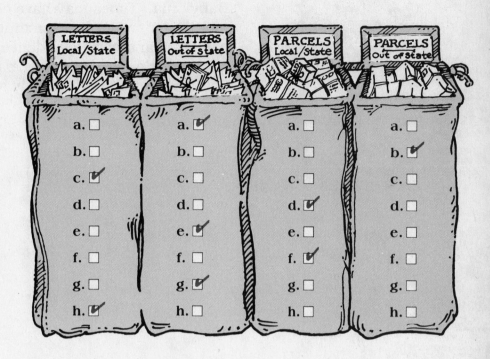

2. You work for a company in Chicago. Upon inspection of the outgoing mail, you notice that several letters do not have zip codes. Use the zip code directory excerpts on the opposite page to find the correct zip codes. On the given lines, write the zip code for each of the following addresses.

a. Chicago Heights, Illinois _____ 60411

b. Chester, Illinois _____ 62233

c. Dunning Station, Chicago, IL _____ 60634

d. Association Building
19 South La Salle
Chicago, IL _____ 60603

e. Bell Telephone
208 West Washington
Chicago, IL _____ 60606

f. Ms. Susana De Guzman
850 Avers Ave. North
Chicago, IL _____ 60651

g. Mr. Wayne Stone
1600 Avers Ave. South
Chicago, IL _____ 60623

h. Balbo Lanes
68 Balbo Ave. East
Chicago, IL _____ 60605

Office Messenger

Reading Maps and Directories

The job of messenger dates back to ancient Egypt and Babylonia. Times may have changed, but the messenger's work has remained the same — to deliver packages and correspondence from one person to another. So the messenger has to know how to get from point A to point B as quickly as possible.

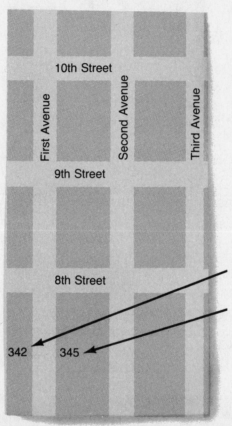

The Street Map

Many messengers have a street map tucked away in their pocket until they become familiar with the city in which they work. At the left is an example of a street map.

Uptown

Building numbers and street numbers get higher.

Downtown

Building numbers and street numbers get lower.

Buildings with even numbers are on one side of the street.

Buildings with odd numbers are on the opposite side of the street.

Will you have to walk uptown or downtown from 9th Street to find 400 First Avenue? <u>downtown</u>

Words to Know

Crosstown — extending across a town, often in an east/west direction

Deliver — to hand over

Downtown — to the business center of a town, usually with lower building and street numbers

Uptown — to the upper part of town, usually with higher building and street numbers

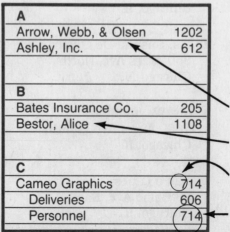

The Building Directory

All building directories list the tenants in alphabetical order. Individuals as well as businesses are often alphabetized together.

company name

individual's name

This is the floor number.

This whole number is the room number.

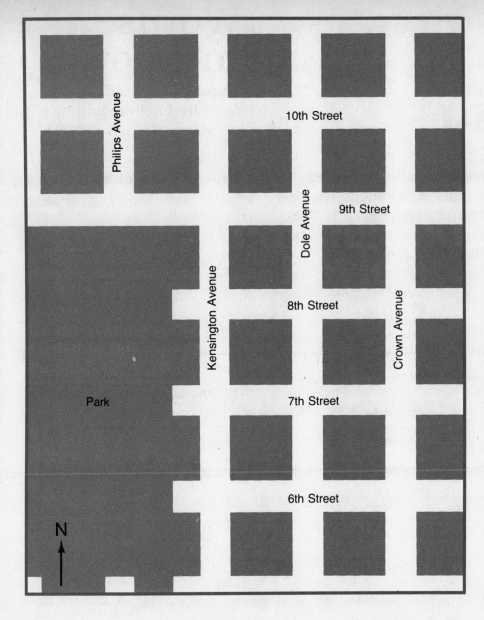

2. Use the street map at the left to answer the following questions. Put a check mark in the box next to the correct answer to each question.

a. You have just picked up a package from an office on Crown Avenue and 6th Street. You have to deliver it to a building on Crown and 10th. Which way will you walk?

❑ downtown
❑ crosstown
☑ uptown

b. Number 715 Kensington is on the right side of the street. Where is 824 Kensington if you remain facing in the same direction?

☑ uptown, left side
❑ downtown, right side
❑ crosstown, left side

c. Number 62 Dole Avenue is between 7th and 8th. Which way would you walk to deliver a letter to 84 Dole Avenue?

☑ uptown
❑ downtown
❑ crosstown

d. You have to make two deliveries; one to a company on Philips and 9th and the other to a studio on Kensington and 6th. You are now on Crown and 9th. What would your route be?

☑ crosstown on 9th to Philips, back to Kensington, and then downtown on Kensington to 6th

❑ uptown to 6th and crosstown to Kensington; then downtown to 9th and one block crosstown to Philips

❑ crosstown on 9th to Kensington and downtown to 6th; then continue crosstown on 6th and uptown on Philips to 9th

1. Refer to the building directory on the opposite page to answer the following questions. Write your answers on the lines provided.

a. You have a large package for Cameo Graphics. What floor will you go to?

7th

b. You must deliver a personal letter to Alice Bestor. What room is she in?

1108

c. You are delivering packages to each company listed in the directory. You want to start from the top floor. Which company should you see first?

Arrow, Webb & Olsen

Receptionist

Taking Telephone Messages

Receptionists handle quite a few telephone calls every day. In addition to giving information to callers, they also have to know how to record information. Receptionists are a lot like newspaper reporters. They're good listeners, they ask the right questions, and they get all the important details.

Tips for Getting Details

● Get the caller's name and the person he or she wishes to speak to.
● Get as many locational details as possible — the caller's company name and/or address and phone number.
● Ask the caller to spell all names. Don't take any spellings for granted.
● Repeat the information as the caller gives it to you. If you don't understand the message, say so.
● Try to get the essential details.
● Verify all information before you hang up.

IS THERE SOMEONE ELSE WHOM YOU CAN SPEAK TO?

WHEN CAN YOU BE REACHED AT THIS NUMBER?

IS THERE ANOTHER NUMBER WHERE YOU CAN BE REACHED?

IS THAT ONE *R* OR TWO?

WHAT IS THIS IN REFERENCE TO?

Recording Details

Who is the message for?

When did the person call?

Who called?

Where can the caller be reached?

Don't forget the area code.

This is the most basic information.

Messages are brief and include only the important details.

Your name

WHILE YOU WERE OUT

To *Mark Stanford*

Date *6/25* Time *10:15*

Name *Eileen Harrow*

of *16 Hill Road Rockville Center*

Phone *(516) 764 - 7289*

☒ telephoned ☒ please call *A.M. only*
☐ returned your call ☐ will call again
☐ wants appointment ☐ urgent

Message *Please send additional research material for art.*

By *Gwen Simmons*

44

1. As the receptionist, you take a call for Mr. Herley. You inform the person that Mr. Herley is not at his desk at the moment. When the caller hears that, she says, "Oh! Well, thank you anyway." What questions should you ask before the caller hangs up?

Would you like to leave

your name and number?

Is there someone else to

whom you can speak?

When can he return your

call?

2. You take a call for Ms. Stetson. The caller tells you his name and the company he represents. He wants Ms. Stetson to return his call as soon as possible. What is the first question you should ask him?

What is the number where you can be reached?

What is the second question you should ask him?

When can you be reached at this number?

3. At 9:15 on November 5, Jack took a message for Mr. Greenway. It is shown at the right. List all the reasons why the message is apt to cause problems for Mr. Greenway when he returns from his board meeting.

WHILE YOU WERE OUT

To _Luther Greenway_

Date _____ Time _____

Name _Diane B._

of _____

Phone _351-0700_

☒ telephoned   ☒ please call
☐ returned your call   ☐ will call again
☐ wants appointment   ☒ urgent

Message _Problem with_
new product you sent her.
New client
By _Jack Seawood_

No date or time, no last name given, no company name

or town where the call originated, no area code.

(Accept all valid answers.)

Vocabulary Review

Many words you learned in this unit have more than one meaning.

1. Read the sentences and decide which meaning of the italicized word is used. Put a check on the line next to your answer.

a. The receptionist was told not to *file* his nails while on the job.

_____ a metal cabinet with drawers

_____ arrange in order, often alphabetically

__✔__ to shape with a file

b. Please pick up a *parcel* from City Hall as soon as possible.

_____ lot

_____ a small part

__✔__ package

c. City Hall is in the *downtown* area, where all the shops are.

_____ south side of town

__✔__ the business center

_____ toward the lower part of town

d. The *local* train stops every ten blocks.

__✔__ makes frequent stops

_____ same town or city

_____ a very limited area

e. If you want your mail to get there fast, don't forget the *zip*!

__✔__ a five-digit number

_____ fast movement

_____ close a zipper

f. At 10th Street, take First Avenue *uptown* to 90th Street.

__✔__ in a direction away from the downtown area

_____ the north side of town

_____ the highest area in town

Reading Skills Review

Use the reading skills you learned in this unit to do the following exercises.

1. Look at the zip code map. Write the zip code for each address below.

a. 50 W. 44th St. _10036_

b. 185 Greenwich Ave. _10011_

c. 201 E. 50th St. _10022_

d. 350 E. 21st St. _10010_

e. 261 W. 28th St. _10001_

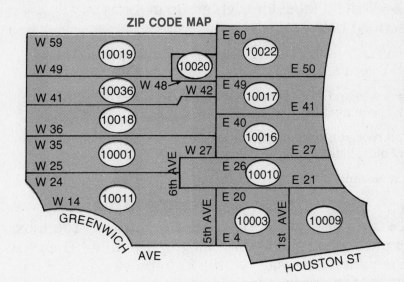

ZIP CODE MAP

2. Suppose you are looking for these buildings and all you know are their zip codes. Use the zip code map to describe their location. Write the correct border street or avenue on the line next to each building name and zip code.

a. Grace Building 10036 _____W 41 to W 48_____

b. One Dag Hammarskjold Plaza 10017 _____E 41 to E 49_____

c. Roosevelt Hospital 10019 _____W 49 to W 59_____

directory

1120 AVENUE OF THE AMERICAS

All-Stat 301
Bingham, Andrew 1946
Buhler Industries 960
Coffee Shop . . . . .Lobby
Crown Pharmacy . . . . .Lobby
Dugan, Janice, C.P.A. 412
Flores, Carol, M.D. 520

3. Find the answer to each question in the building directory.

a. Suppose you are delivering packages to everyone listed in the directory. You want to start from the top. Whom should you see first?

Andrew Bingham

b. The doctor is on the __5th__ floor in room number ____520____.

c. Which company will you find on the third floor?

All-Stat

Writing Skills Review

Use your writing skills to do the following exercises.

1. Write a label for each group of items described below.

a. mail to customers, letters from clients, letters to and from other companies

b. notes to and from people working in the same office, reminders from the managers

c. toll receipts, transportation vouchers, restaurant checks, hotel bills, lists of travel expenses

d. names and addresses of clients in the Western Region

Correspondence

Inter-office Memorandums

Expenses

Clients, Western Region

2. Suppose you work in a doctor's office. You took this phone call. Read the dialogue carefully. Then write the telephone message on the form provided. The time is noon and the date is today.

Caller: Hello. Is Dr. Velez in?

You: Yes, he is, but he's busy with a patient at this moment. May I know who's calling?

Caller: I'm Vivian Chen.

You: Is that V-I-V-I-A-N C-H-E-N?

Caller: That's right.

You: May I have your address and phone number please?

Caller: 22 Lake Drive. 555-9424.

You: Would you like to leave a message?

Caller: Oh, yes. I'm the doctor's good friend and former neighbor. We grew up together, you know. Please tell the doctor that I have just come back from a great tour of Africa. It was really wonderful! I'd like to see him soon. Please ask him to call me back as soon as possible.

WHILE YOU WERE OUT

To *Doctor Velez*

Date *(today's date)*   Time *12:00 n*

Name *Vivian Chen*

of *22 Lake Drive*

Phone *555-9424*

☑ telephoned   ☑ please call
☐ returned your call   ☐ will call again
☐ wants appointment   ☐ urgent

Message *has just returned from Africa, would like to see you soon*

By *(student's signature)*

Unit 4

Specialized Office Jobs

Some office jobs require special training. Office machine operators, keyboarders or typists, stenographers, and secretaries usually take special business courses to do their jobs. Equally essential to these jobs are reading and writing skills — following directions, locating and evaluating information, proofreading, using context clues, syllabication, punctuation, capitalization, and letter writing. This unit is designed to help you develop and practice these important reading and writing skills.

Copying Machine Operator

Following Directions

Copying machines are used in many offices to duplicate paper. These machines are easy to operate, as long as you follow the instructions.

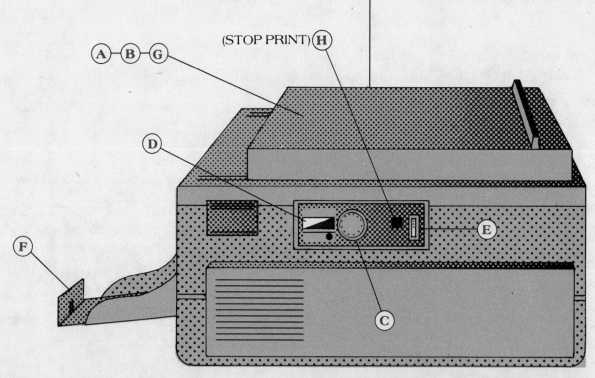

(STOP PRINT) H

1. Write the letter of the correct answer.

a. Which part of the diagram is NOT mentioned in the instructions? **H**

b. How can you make copies lighter or darker? **D**

c. What step tells you how to place the original on the machine? **B**

d. Which button sets the machine in motion? **E**

e. To make more than one copy, which step should you follow? **C**

Copying Instructions

A Lift cover.

B Place original face down and close cover.

C Dial number of copies.

D Set light/dark lever.

E Press START PRINT.

F Look for copies in tray.

G Lift cover and remove original.

2. Although each office copier is a little different, some operating steps are common. This diagram of another type of copier comes with an incomplete set of instructions. Complete each step.

Operating Instructions for Copying Machine

a. Press button marked POWER ON.

b. Lift _____ *cover* _____.

c. Place original _____ *face down* _____.

d. Set the _____ *light/dark lever* _____ to the desired darkness.

e. Close _____ *cover* _____.

f. To make more than one copy, _____ *turn the copy dial to the* _____ *number of copies desired* _____.

g. Press _____ *print* _____ button.

h. Get copy or copies from _____ *tray* _____.

i. Lift cover and _____ *remove original* _____.

j. Press button marked _____ *power off* _____.

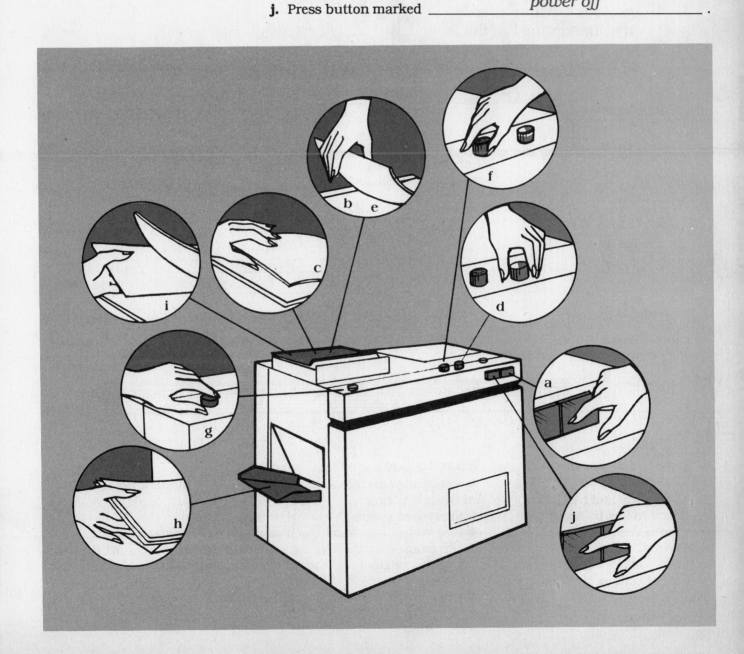

Word Processing Operator

Proofreading

Fast fingers aren't enough. You need sharp eyes to spot any spelling and punctuation mistakes. You also have to reread carefully for items that were omitted or keyboarded incorrectly.

When you proofread, you look back and forth from the original to the typed copy to make sure they are both the same.

Did you catch the three mistakes?

When you proof read you look back and fourth from the

Tips

for Proofreading

● Read slowly and carefully.
● Proofread line by line, comparing the original with your typed copy.
● When you are not sure of the spelling of certain words, use the dictionary.

What to Look For

● something omitted, such as a punctuation mark, a word, or even an entire sentence
● misspelled words
● incorrect punctuation, such as a semicolon instead of a comma
● correction — Is the spacing similar? Are the paragraphs the same in both the original and the copy? Were any items typed either above or below the line?
● errors in typing or keyboarding numbers

1. Compare the original and its keyboarded copy shown below. Look for spelling and punctuation mistakes. In the space above each line, write the correct spelling of each misspelled word. Add any missing punctuation, and cross out those marks that should not be there. The first line has been done for you.

Within the ~~nezt~~ *next* two ~~decaeds,~~ *decades* computers that ~~sieak~~ *speak* will be

~~comon~~ *common* in American homes and offices. The public is ~~all~~

~~ready~~ *already* accustomed to hearing ~~compyter boices~~ *computer voices* when ~~call~~ *calling*

the telephone company for time ̭ temperature, and

~~westher~~ *weather* reports ⊙ Many business firms use ~~qudio~~ *audio* output

systems for credit ~~verifacation~~ *verification* and financial calculations.

Since technology ~~haw~~ *has* progressed to the point where

audio response ~~sound~~ *sounds* almost natural ⸞ a vastly wider

market for these ~~compuers~~ *computers* can be ~~perdicted,~~ *predicted* ⊙

Within the next two decades, computers that speak will be common in American homes and offices. The public is already accustomed to hearing computer voices when calling the telephone company for time, temperature, and weather reports. Many business firms use audio output systems for credit verification and financial calculations. Since technology has progressed to the point where audio response sounds almost natural, a vastly wider market for these computers can be predicted.

2. You have keyboarded the following list of addresses from a handwritten page. There are many different kinds of mistakes. Find the mistakes and write the corrections in the space on the right.

Mr. Ricardo Cruz
645 Oak Dr.
Wise, VA 24293

Ms. Nellie Talmidge
2230 Goshen Rd.
Tupelo, MS 38801

Ms. E. Waltham
18 Spring Ct.
Rutland, VT. 05701

Ms. Mary Ann Frank
1112 Ashtree Ln.
Belle Plaine, KS 52208

Ms. Dell Paxton
250 Heath St.
Rainbow City, AL 35901

Mr. Jack Soo
Marble Mnr.
Ellensburg, WA 98926

Mr. D. Martin Oggs
15 Breaker Rd.
Anchorage, AK 99501

Mr. ~~Richardo~~ Cruz — *Ricardo*
645 Oak Dr.
Wise, VA 24293 — *Ms.*
— *Rutland*
~~Mrs.~~ E. Waltham
18 Spring Ct.
~~Rutlanf,~~ VT 05701
— *Ms. Dell Paxton*
— *250 Heath St.*
— *Rainbow City, Al*
— *35901*
Mr. Martin Oggs
~~015~~ Breaker Rd. — *D.*
Anchorage, AK 99501

Ms. Nellie ~~Talmadge~~ — *Talmidge*
~~22-30~~ Goshen Rd. — *2230*
Tupelo, ~~Miss. 33801~~ — *MS 38801*
Ms. ~~Maryanna~~ Frank — (add space)
112 Ashtree Ln.
Belle ~~Plain, KA~~ 52208 — *Mary Ann*
— *Plaine, KS*
Mr. Jack Soo
Marble Mnr.
~~Ellenburg,~~ WA ~~98826~~ — *Ellensburg 98926*

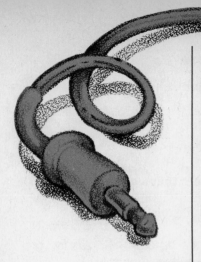

Word Processing Operator

Typing from Dictation

The use of dictating equipment demands an important skill. The keyboarder must be able to identify sound-alike words, those that have the same sound but have different meanings and spellings.

1. You have just typed this letter from a dictating machine. Proofread it for mistakes and for sound-alike words. Cross out the incorrect word, and write the correct form in the space directly above it.

Words to Know

This is a partial list of the most commonly confused sound-alike words.

compliment — a flattering remark
complement — the amount needed to make a thing complete

fourth — 4th
forth — ahead, toward

it's — a short form of *it is*
its — a word used to show ownership

there — a place
their — a word used to show ownership
they're — a short form of *they are*

too — also
to — toward; a word often used before verbs
two — the number (2)

54

THE EXETER CORPORATION
San Francisco, CA 94515

July 15, 1991

Mr. Lex Green
109 South Cornell
Columbus, Ohio 43216

Dear Mr. Green:

 your
Thank you for ~~you're~~ letter of July 9. We do not have all the

 ⊙ *However*
materials you ordered in stock, ~~however~~, we expect a shipment

 two
within the next ~~too~~ weeks. At the present time, we will be

 to *principal*
pleased ~~two~~ send a partial order consisting of the ~~principle~~

 your
items as indicated on ~~you're~~ list. The remainder will be

forthcoming *by*
~~fourth-coming~~ as soon as it's made available to us ~~buy~~ our

supplier.

 for
Kindly remit your check ~~four~~ the total by return mail. Note

 there
that ~~their~~ is a small shipping charge.

Sincerely,

Anita Perez

Anita Perez,
Customer Service

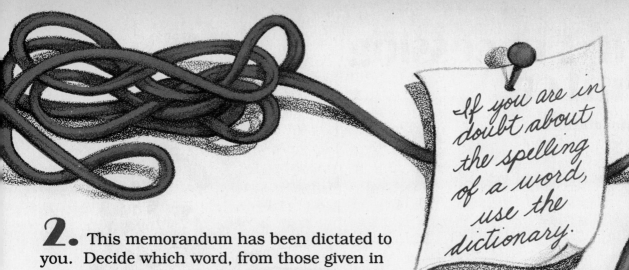

If you are in doubt about the spelling of a word, use the dictionary.

2. This memorandum has been dictated to you. Decide which word, from those given in parentheses, correctly completes each sentence. Use the dictionary if you need help.

MEMORANDUM

To: The Sales Department   September 16, 1992
From: Michael Beardsley
Re: Sales for the ____*fourth*____ (forth, fourth) quarter

I am pleased ____*to*____ (to, too, two) announce that ____*there*____ (their, they're, there) has been a sharp increase in sales for the ____*fourth*____ (forth, fourth) quarter over last year's figures. Attached is a list that ____*breaks*____ (breaks, brakes) down the ____*principal*____ (principle, principal) accounts by geographical area. I wish ____*to*____ (to, too, two) extend my ____*compliments*____ (complements, compliments) to each and every one of you for ____*your*____ (you're, your) outstanding efforts in the field.

Doris McKesson has been named head of the Atlanta office, ____*where*____ (where, wear) she will replace Rodney Taylor, who is retiring. Elena Torres assumes Ms. McKesson's position.

Finally, the New Products Division reports several thousand dollars worth of advance orders for ____*its*____ (it's, its) North Country heating unit, thanks ____*to*____ (to, too, two) the enthusiasm generated ____*by*____ (by, buy) Robert Knowles and Philip Babcock.

Word Processing Operator

Finding Information

The following dialogue will give you an idea of what important skills are needed to succeed as a word processing operator.

INT.   What skills should someone have to become a word processing trainee?

JASON: You should be able to type between 50 and 60 words per minute. Your grammar and spelling skills must be good. Knowing how to use a dictionary and other reference materials is important, too. But if you want to get ahead, you need to apply other special work skills. As a matter of fact, I've been working toward a promotion and expect it soon.

INT.   What are some of the traits and special work skills needed to get ahead?

JASON: Teamwork is important here. Personnel must often help each other, for example, when someone is at a meeting or absent. The work must still be done. Also, you may be taken off one assignment and put on another with a higher priority. So, flexibility is important, too.

INT.   Teamwork and flexibility are not word processing skills, are they?

JASON: No, but they are *traits* you need to succeed in the word processing department of this and most companies.

Words to Know

Flexibility — being able to change quickly

Teamwork — working together

Trainee — a person who is learning on the job

Word processing — using a computer to type, store, and edit information

56

a. What are the three skills needed to become a word processing trainee?

type 50-60 words per minute

good grammar and spelling skills

know how to use reference materials

b. What are the two traits needed for getting ahead in word processing?

team work

flexibility

1. Read the interview with Jason on page 56 to find the answers to questions **a** and **b**. Write your answers on the given lines.

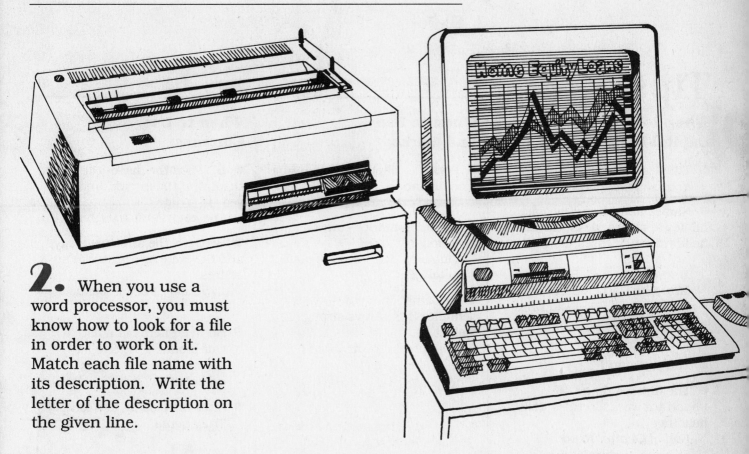

2. When you use a word processor, you must know how to look for a file in order to work on it. Match each file name with its description. Write the letter of the description on the given line.

_d___ Fourth Quarter Sales

_b___ Supply Request

_c___ Customer List

_a___ Travel Plans

_e___ Expense Report

a. a listing of when and where someone will be while traveling

b. a letter asking for computer paper and other supplies

c. a list of people who buy goods from the store

d. a report of how much was sold during the last 3 months of a given year

e. a list of expenses

Stenographer

Punctuation and Capitalization

A stenographer must transcribe shorthand notes into clear, typewritten form. That's why good punctuation and capitalization skills are essential.

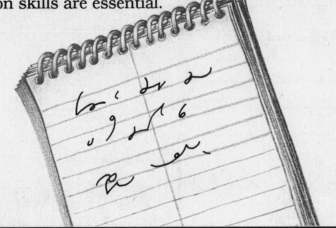

Words to Know

Shorthand — a faster way of writing notes, especially from dictation

Transcribe — to make a written copy of (dictated information or shorthand notes)

Tips

When to Use Capital Letters:

- The first word in a sentence
  Your shipment is on its way.

- Names and titles of people, names of places, days, months, holidays, businesses, and organizations

Mr. Santos	*Halloween*
Mrs. Etta Carr	*San Antonio*
Wednesday	*Viola Drive*
Amex Company	
Steno Society	

- The pronoun *I*

- The first word and all important words in titles and headings
  End of Quarter Report
  Sales Summary for the Month of June

When to Use End Marks:

- Period — after a statement or a command
  Please attend the meeting.

- Question mark — after a question
  May we have a copy of your catalog?

- Exclamation point — after a sentence that shows strong feeling
  Your products are great!

When to Use Commas:

- Between the day of the week, the day of the month, and the year in a date
  Tuesday, April 10, 1990

- Between the street, the city, and the state or country in an address
  275 King Street, Topeka, Kansas

- Between items in a list
  Our products include file cabinets, desks, tables, and chairs.

- After the closing in a letter
  Truly yours,

1. Rewrite the following sentences. Use capital letters and punctuation marks correctly.

a. the next meeting will be at 50 main street asbury park new jersey on friday october 20, 1990

The next meeting will be at 50 Main Street, Asbury Park, New Jersey, on Friday, October 20, 1990.

Begin the first word of every sentence with a capital letter.

b. the manufacturing department reports a 20% increase in the cost
of materials labor and energy

<u>The Manufacturing Department reports a 20% increase</u>

<u>in the cost of materials, labor, and energy.</u>

c. have you checked the entries in the cash record

<u>Have you checked the entries in the cash record?</u>

<u> </u>

2. Use punctuation and capitalization skills to make this letter more readable. Rewrite each line.

pax travel agency

9131 queens blvd

elmhurst new york 11373

march 3 1990

dr karen mason

201 eagle street

alexandria virginia 22306

dear dr mason:

thank you for your

letter of february

15 1990 we have

several tours to

africa that include

the game preserves

the departure dates

are june 15 july 10

august 4 and september 2

may we serve you soon

sincerely yours

l t jones

<u>Pax Travel Agency</u>

<u>91-31 Queens Blvd.</u>

<u>Elmhurst, NY 11373</u>

<u>March 3, 1990</u>

<u>Dr. Karen Mason</u>

<u>201 Eagle Street</u>

<u>Alexandria, Virginia 22306</u>

<u>Dear Dr. Mason:</u>

<u>Thank you for your letter of February 15,</u>
<u>1990. We have several tours to Africa that</u>
<u>include the game preserves. The departure</u>
<u>dates are June 15, July 10, August 4 and</u>
<u>September 2.</u>

<u>May we serve you soon?</u>

<u>Sincerely yours,</u>

<u>L. T. Jones</u>

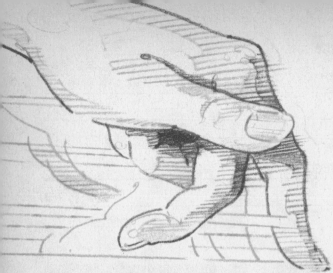

Secretary | Tips

Using the Yellow Pages

Secretaries must know how to type and take dictation, but they have other responsibilities as well. Fact-finding is one of their duties, and the Yellow Pages of the telephone book often provide much needed information.

Suppose you have to arrange for the fast delivery of a special package. Here's how the Yellow Pages can help.

● First, locate the listings for the type of business or service you need. Delivery services are listed under the heading *Delivery*.
● Then, look at the display ads for additional information.

> # *A L E R T*
> # *D E L I V E R Y*
>
> —**Express service to the business world in all of North America**
> —**OVERNIGHT DELIVERY:**
>   land & air
> —**Low, low rates**
> ## 555-4098 38-21 Mercury Ave.

A display ad includes: the name of the company

details

the phone number and address

● Last, compare several display ads. Decide which company seems to provide the kinds of services you need. Start calling!

Words to Know

Display ads — paid announcements of goods or services

Yellow Pages — a section in the telephone book that alphabetically lists names, telephone numbers, and addresses under a type of business, service, or profession

1. Answer YES or NO. Write the line from the ad that tells why.

a. Can you send a package from Chicago to Albuquerque through Alert Delivery? *Yes. Express Service to the business world in all of North America.*

b. Would you use Alert Delivery if you needed to send a package by sea? *No. Alert delivers only by land and air.*

2. Part of your job as a secretary is to arrange hotel accomodations. Read and compare these display ads from the Yellow Pages. Then answer each question below.

a. The branch managers need rooms for a night to meet with the staff in the midtown office. Which number should you call?

555-1370

b. A quick business meeting is planned. Out-of-town sales agents will fly in and out the same day. Which number should you call?

555-3715

c. You have to arrange a three-day business conference in a relaxing atmosphere. Which number should you call?

555-2374

d. Are all these hotels air-conditioned?

No

e. Your company is entertaining some foreigners who like to enjoy the city during off-hours. Which hotel should you reserve for them?

Hotel America

514 HOTELS

HOMETOWN HOTEL

*color TV
*restaurant
*air-conditioned
*heated pool
*meeting rooms
*convention facilities
*all major credit cards accepted

5 MINUTES FROM AIRPORT
555-3715
284-26 Rockaway Blvd.

HOTEL AMERICA

*convenient midtown location
*2 blocks from Central Station
*500 rooms — TV — telephone

*air-conditioned
*gourmet dining at The Pub
*near theaters and business areas

619 Main Street   **555-1370**

North Shore Inn

Northern Parkway & Route 106
Northtown
555-2374

*quiet country atmosphere
*woods, trees, beach
*meeting rooms
*pool, health facilities
*color TV *dining room

Vocabulary Review

1. You have just learned how the following words are used in specialized office jobs. Now use the words to complete the sentences at the right.

accuracy
diagram
display ads
hyphen
instructions
margins
original
print
quantity
shorthand
syllables
transcribe
typing speed
Yellow Pages

a. The machine's _____diagram_____ shows its different parts.

b. Follow the operating _____instructions_____ on the inside cover of the machine.

c. You can't make good copies if the _____original_____ is barely readable.

d. To take dictation easily, you must be able to write _____shorthand_____ .

e. A word can be divided between _____syllables_____ .

f. Look for the telephone number of Korean Airlines under *Airlines* in the _____Yellow Pages_____ .

g. If your company wants to announce its services in the newspapers or in the Yellow Pages, it can use _____display ads_____ .

h. Avoid typing off the page; set your _____margins_____ .

i. If you type 90 WPM, your _____typing speed_____ is above average.

2. Decide which word, from those given in parentheses, correctly completes each sentence in the letter.

Brooks

Department Store 121 E. 8th St., Austin, Texas 78701

June 6, 1993

Ms. Laura Trager
101 South Cornell
Elgin, Oregon 97827

Dear Ms. Trager:

Thank you for ordering ___two___ (two, too, to) special sale sweaters. ___They're___ (There, They're, Their) out of stock ___here___ (here, hear) in the store, but we will be receiving a new supply soon. We will ___write___ (right, write) to let you know.

Sincerely,

Joseph Brooks

Reading Skills Review

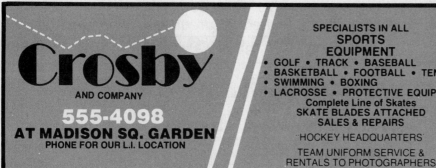
1. The ad and telephone listing above are from the Yellow Pages of a local telephone directory. Read these carefully and answer questions **a**, **b**, and **c**.

a. If you need to buy a soccer ball, which number should you call?

555-2274

b. Your hockey team needs to have new skate blades attached to old skates. Which company should you call?

Crosby and Company

c. A new company, Step-Rite Inc., sells jogging shoes. Will it be listed in this section of the Yellow Pages? *Yes, between Sports Warehouse and Sun Sporting Goods.*

2. This set of instructions comes from a typewriter's operating manual. Read it carefully and answer questions **d**, **e**, and **f**.

d. Which part should you space out of the way before moving the left margin stop? *pointer*

e. What two movements are required to set the margin stops? *push in* and *slide*

f. Why would you press the margin release key? *Press the margin release to type past the margin.*

To Set the Margins

Push in and slide the margin stops to the new margin settings.

The left margin stop cannot be moved past the red pointer. Space the pointer out of the way before moving the margin stop.

The right margin stop prevents you from typing past the right margin; however, you can space or tab through it. To type past the right margin, press the margin release key and continue typing.

Writing Skills Review

1. Rewrite the sentences on the right. Use correct punctuation marks and capital letters.

a. you are cordially invited to attend our thanksgiving dinner at 25 colorado blvd on thursday, november 25

You are cordially invited to attend our Thanksgiving dinner at 25 Colorado Blvd. on Thursday, November 25.

b. thank you for your kind attention i look forward to hearing from you soon

Thank you for your kind attention. I look forward to hearing from you soon.

2. As you type a letter, some words are falling off the line. Use a hyphen to show where each word can be divided.

in February	*Feb-*
our products	*prod-*
the delivery	*de-*
continuously	*contin-*
is operating	*oper-*

3. Rewrite this business letter on the office stationery.

december 12 1990

ms. carol wirth
22-78 31 place
forest hills n y 11375

dear ms wirth

congratulations
your interview
was a big success
and you've got
the job you start
monday at nine
if you have any
questions please
call me

yours truly

helen coleman
personnel manager

Scholastic Inc.
730 Broadway
New York, NY 10003
(212) 505-3026

Scholastic

December 12, 1990

Ms. Carol Wirth
22-78 31 Place
Forest Hills, N Y 11375

Dear Ms. Wirth:

Congratulations! Your interview was a big success and you've got the job. You start Monday at nine.
If you have any questions, please call me.

Yours truly,
Helen Coleman
Personnel Manager

Unit 5

Service Jobs

When your job is designed to serve people, you are engaged in a service occupation. The work involves doing something that people cannot easily do on their own, or prefer not to do themselves. Sample jobs in this unit practice important reading and writing skills. You will read signs, symbols, road maps, menus, and brochures. You will recognize cause and effect, draw conclusions, summarize, outline, and write clear sentences.

Chauffeur

Knowing Road Signs

A person who drives for a living — a chauffeur — must know and obey signs. Life and livelihood may depend on them.

Road signs are important to you too, whether you want to be a chauffeur or not.

The Shape is the Clue
- A stop sign is an eight-sided figure.
- The yield sign is a triangle.
- A warning sign is diamond-shaped.
- A square or rectangular sign gives a rule or direction.
- A slash means no.

The Secret Code of Interstate Routes
- East-west routes have even numbers.
- North-south routes have odd numbers.
- When a route sign has a three-digit number, the first digit is the key.

An even number means the route goes *around* the city.

An odd number means the route goes *into* a city.

Some Important Signs or Symbols and What They Mean

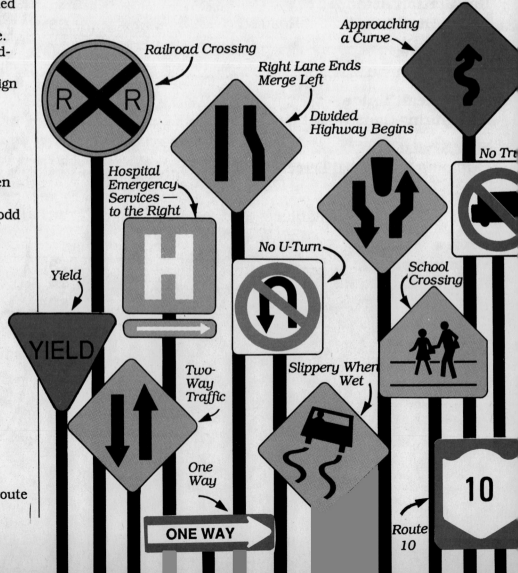

Railroad Crossing

Right Lane Ends Merge Left

Approaching a Curve

Divided Highway Begins

No Tr[u]

Hospital Emergency Services — to the Right

No U-Turn

School Crossing

Yield

Slippery When Wet

Two-Way Traffic

One Way

ONE WAY

Route 10

10

66

1. Match the signs or symbols with the shapes and meanings. First, choose the correct shape for each traffic or road sign symbol. Write the letter for the correct shape on the given line next to each symbol. Then, draw lines to connect symbols with their meanings. Number 3 has been done for you.

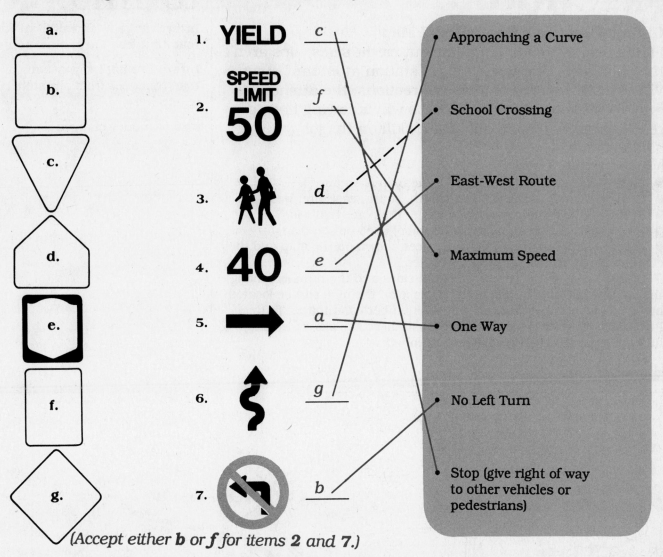

a.

b.

c.

d.

e.

f.

g.

1. **YIELD**   _c_

2. **SPEED LIMIT 50**   _f_

3. (pedestrian symbol)   _d_

4. **40**   _e_

5. (arrow)   _a_

6. (curve symbol)   _g_

7. (no left turn)   _b_

• Approaching a Curve

• School Crossing

• East-West Route

• Maximum Speed

• One Way

• No Left Turn

• Stop (give right of way to other vehicles or pedestrians)

*(Accept either **b** or **f** for items **2** and **7**.)*

2. Study each picture carefully. What symbol or symbols will apply to each picture? First, print or draw the symbol inside each correct shape. Then, write the meaning of that symbol on the given line.

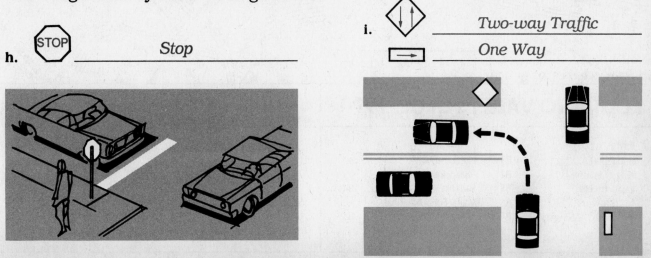

h. (STOP)   *Stop*

i. (two-way symbol)   *Two-way Traffic*

(one way symbol)   *One Way*

Gas Station Attendant

Giving Directions from a Road Map

Filling up gas tanks and filling out credit sales slips aren't the only tasks that keep the gas station attendant busy. When travelers stop to ask for directions, the attendant must be able to give them. That's why knowing how to read a road map is an important skill on the job.

Map Reading Tools

- **Title** — gives you an idea of what the map is about.
- **Compass Rose** — shows where north, south, east, and west are.
- **Scale** — tells exactly how much larger the place really is.
- **Key** — tells the meaning of each symbol used on the map.
- **Index** — alphabetically lists the places shown on the map and the coordinates by which they can be located.
- **Coordinates** — the letters along the sides and the numbers along the top and bottom of a map. Every place on the map can be located by using one letter coordinate and one number coordinate. To find Plymouth Valley on A4, for example, read down the side of the map to find the letter A. Then read across to column 4.

Read this map.

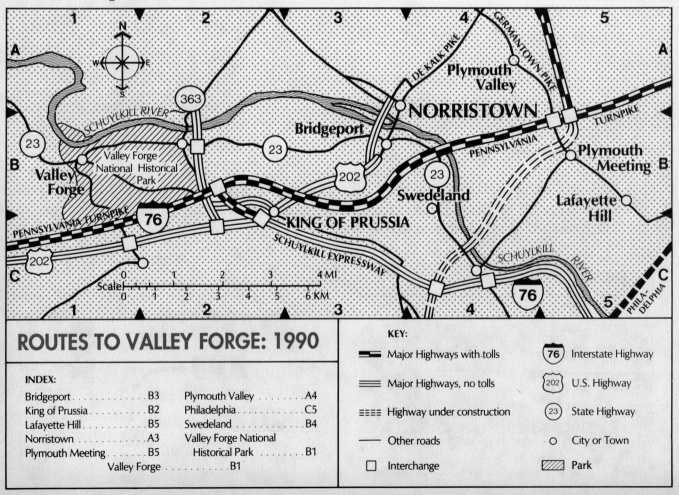

ROUTES TO VALLEY FORGE: 1990

KEY:

- ▬▬ Major Highways with tolls
- ═══ Major Highways, no tolls
- ≡≡≡≡ Highway under construction
- —— Other roads
- ☐ Interchange
- **76** Interstate Highway
- **202** U.S. Highway
- **23** State Highway
- ○ City or Town
- ▨ Park

1. Use the map-reading tools and the map on the opposite page to answer these questions.

a. Judging from the title, you can tell that this map is especially helpful to people going to _____*Valley Forge*_____ .

b. The compass rose tells you that Valley Forge is located _____*west*_____ of Plymouth Meeting.

c. Swedeland is about ___*one*___ mile(s) away from the Pennsylvania Turnpike.

d. Would you pay toll on route 202? ___*No*___

e. What are the letter/number coordinates for Philadelphia? ___*C5*___

2. Suppose you work at a gas station in Plymouth Valley. How would you answer these questions from your customers?

a. What direction should I take to get to the Pennsylvania Turnpike?
_____*South on Germantown Pike*_____

b. How far is Plymouth Meeting from here? ___*about 2 miles*___

c. What roads should I take to get to Valley Forge as fast as possible? ___*Germantown Pike*___ and ___*Penn. Turnpike*___

d. Do I have to pay a toll if I take the Pennsylvania Turnpike? ___*Yes*___

e. In which direction from the Pennsylvania Turnpike is Lafayette Hill located? _____*southeast*_____

3. Give specific directions to these travelers.

a. The Cohen family, who wants to go from Swedeland to Valley Forge without having to pay tolls.
___*Take Route 23 north, then west.*___

b. Mr. and Mrs. Reyes, who want to get to Plymouth Meeting from Valley Forge as fast as possible.
South to Penn. Turnpike, east to
Germantown Pike and south to
Plymouth Meeting.

Food Server

Reading a Menu

A customer walks into a restaurant hoping to eat pot roast. He reads the menu, but can't find the dish listed.

"Sir," you say, "we do have pot roast. It is written as *sauerbraten* on the menu."

It is important for a food server to know the foreign words or phrases which are used to name certain foods or desserts. Customers often ask what the foreign food terms mean.

Tips

Follow these tips and the tip (the money kind) will follow.
● Read the menu carefully.
● If you don't know a term on the menu, ask someone who knows.
● Memorize the dishes and the prices.

Words to Know

A la Carte — dish by dish from the menu, each with a stated price

Appetizer — a small portion of food served before the main dish

Dinner — a full meal for which one price is charged

Entree — main course or dish

Filet — boneless meat or dish

Goulash — beef or veal stew

Sauteed — fried quickly in shallow fat

Strudel — pastry with light flaky dough and fruit filling

Wiener schnitzel — breaded veal cutlet

Menu

APPETIZERS *$5.25 each*

Fruit Cocktail	Little Neck Clams
Shrimp Cocktail	Baked Stuffed Clams

SOUP *$3.75 each*

Lentil
Clam Chowder
Chicken with Asparagus

TOSSED GREEN SALAD *$3.10*

ENTREES

		DINNER	A LA CARTE
Broiled Filet of Flounder		$ 18.95	$ 14.95
Baked Brook Trout	Dinner is	19.95	15.95
Sauteed Bay Scallops	served with	18.50	14.65
Lobster Tail	choice of	21.85	17.70
Broiled Chopped Sirloin Steak	*appetizer	18.95	15.35
Broiled Short Ribs of Beef	*soup	18.50	14.50
Hungarian Beef Goulash	*salad	18.50	15.00
Sauteed Calf's Liver	*potato	19.25	15.50
Roast Duck	*vegetables	19.25	15.50
Sauerbraten	*dessert	19.50	15.75
Wiener Schnitzel	*beverage	19.50	15.75

DESSERTS *$4.65 each*

Cheesecake	Cake and Ice Cream	Melon in Season
Apple Strudel	Seven Layer Cake	Ice Cream Nut Roll

Coffee, Tea, or Milk . . . $ 0.90

Use the menu on the opposite page to do the following exercises.

1. You take an order for:

a. Lobster tail a la carte. Will you include a dessert?

No

b. A pot roast dinner. How much will you charge?

$19.50

c. A veal cutlet dinner. Which item on the menu will you serve?

Wiener Schnitzel

d. One beef stew a la carte. How much does it cost?

$15.00

2. A customer orders shrimp cocktail, lobster tail, mixed vegetables, apple strudel, and coffee. You are the food server. Fill out this check:

GUEST RECEIPT	
Description	**Price**
Shrimp Cocktail	*5.25*
Lobster Tail (mixed veg.)	*17.70*
Apple Strudel	*4.65*
Coffee	*.90*
Total	*28.50*
Please pay cashier	

3. Suppose you're a food server at the restaurant whose menu is on the opposite page. Each customer described below asks you to suggest an entire dinner. Write down your choice on the given line next to each course.

a. The customer doesn't eat seafood or fowl, and doesn't want ice cream or pastry.

Appetizer or soup: *Fruit cocktail*

Entree: *Sirloin Steak, short ribs, beef goulash, or calf's liver*

Dessert: *Melon in season*

b. The customer wants fresh clams, boneless fish, and pastry with fruit filling.

Appetizer or soup: *Little neck clams*

Entree: *Broiled filet of flounder*

Dessert: *Apple strudel*

c. The customer likes fowl and cheese.

Appetizer or soup: *Chicken with asparagus*

Entree: *Roast duck*

Dessert: *Cheesecake*

Home Health Aide

Recognizing Cause and Effect

Suppose you are a home health aide. Your job is to take care of people who are recovering from illnesses at home. You might serve meals, help make the patient comfortable, and carry out the doctor's orders. You are also expected to take charge when someone in the house is suddenly injured or becomes ill. Before the doctor arrives, the victim's life may depend on your first-aid skills.

Tips for Finding Cause and Effect

● A "why" question states the effect. The answer states the cause.

Effect: Why is the victim *choking?*
Cause: There is a *foreign object in the person's throat.*

● These are some of the words or phrases that indicate cause and effect relationships:

because	*due to*	*on account of*
the result of	*the outcome of*	*the reason for*

● In a series of actions or events, an effect may be a cause of the next event.

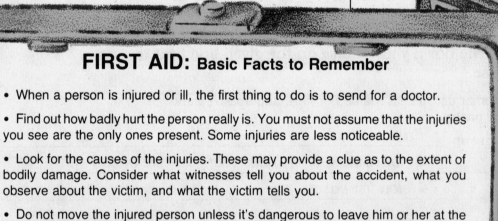

FIRST AID: Basic Facts to Remember

• When a person is injured or ill, the first thing to do is to send for a doctor.

• Find out how badly hurt the person really is. You must not assume that the injuries you see are the only ones present. Some injuries are less noticeable.

• Look for the causes of the injuries. These may provide a clue as to the extent of bodily damage. Consider what witnesses tell you about the accident, what you observe about the victim, and what the victim tells you.

• Do not move the injured person unless it's dangerous to leave him or her at the accident site. Apply such first aid as is possible until more highly qualified medical personnel arrive.

• In all your actions, be careful not to move the victim any more than necessary to support life. Unnecessary movements might worsen unseen fractures or spinal injuries. Mishandled spinal injury, for example, could cause paralysis.

• While there are many conditions that can cause death, impaired breathing and too much bleeding require attention first. Then focus on other obvious injuries — open wounds should be sealed, fractures immobilized, burns covered, and less serious bleeding wounds dressed.

• Next, do a secondary survey — a head-to-toe examination. Start with the victim's head, then neck, trunk, arms, and legs. Look for swelling, discoloration, lumps, and tenderness. These might indicate unseen injuries.

1. Decide whether each cause and effect statement below is true or false. Write T or F on the line.

_F_ **a.** You apply first aid because you know better than the doctor present at the accident site.

_T_ **b.** Difficulty in breathing should be treated first because it is a condition that may kill the victim.

_T_ **c.** Paralysis may result from a spinal injury that is handled wrong.

_F_ **d.** When a person becomes ill, move him or her to a safe place and apply first aid.

_T_ **e.** Swelling and discoloration indicate hidden injuries.

2. Write a complete cause and effect sentence to answer each question.

a. Why should you look for the causes of an injury?

The cause may provide a clue as to the extent of this injury.

b. Why shouldn't you move the victim unnecessarily while applying first aid?

Unnecessary movements may worsen unseen fractures of spinal injuries.

3. Sometimes, a cause tells you what the effect will be. What is the most likely effect of each of these events? Check the best answer.

a. You immerse a slightly burned finger in cold water.

❏ skin blisters   ☑ pain stops   ❏ finger freezes

b. You cover an open wound with the cleanest cloth you can find.

❏ wound bleeds   ❏ blood darkens   ☑ bleeding stops

c. You flush the eye with clean water.

☑ foreign object is removed   ❏ eye becomes red   ❏ foreign object moves to upper lid

4. Sometimes, the effects help you determine the causes. What is the most likely cause of each condition?

a. Itching, moderate swelling, and redness of a small area on your arm.

☑ insect bite   ❏ frostbite   ❏ snakebite

b. Unusual shape, swelling, discoloration, grating sound, exposed bone, and pain in a leg.

❏ sprain   ☑ fracture   ❏ paralysis

73

Hair Stylist

Outlining Sequential Directions

Often, the directions for using a hair product are too complex to remember. The hair stylist must be able to recognize the main and in-between steps of a process and outline them in sequence.

Here's your chance to sharpen your outlining skills on the job as a hair stylist.

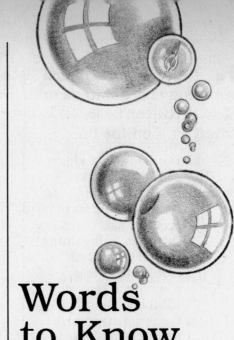

Words to Know

Lathering — forming foam

Neutralizer — used to stop a chemical reaction

Outline — to show the important features or different parts of written directions or instructions

Sequence — order

Tips for Outlining Complex Directions

● Write a title. It should say the purpose of the directions.
● Identify the main steps and number them in sequence. Use roman numerals.
● Identify the in-between or smaller steps under the main steps. List them in sequence. Use capital letters to differentiate them from the main steps.

---

1. Read the directions in paragraph form. Then study the outline that a hair stylist made. Write the last two smaller steps on the given lines.

DIRECTIONS:
HONEY PLUS is a two-step process of shampooing and conditioning hair. First, shampoo the hair by applying the pink liquid on wet hair, lathering it, and then rinsing with warm water. Next, condition the hair by applying the yellow liquid on shampooed hair. Rinse after waiting for five minutes. Towel dry the hair.

Outline:

Using Honey Plus ⟩ *title*

I. Shampoo. ⟩ *main step*

   A. Wet hair.

   B. Apply pink liquid. ⟩ *in-between steps*

   C. Lather.

   D. Rinse.

II. Condition

   A. Apply yellow liquid.

   B. Wait five minutes.

   C. _Rinse._

   D. _Towel dry._

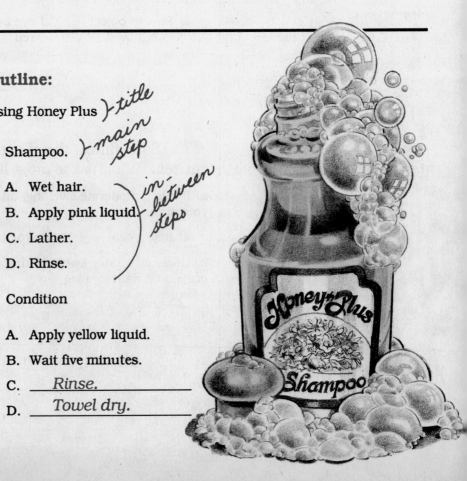

2. A professional hair stylist certainly wants to satisfy the customer. The important tips on the right will help make sure the job is done right.

Read each paragraph and fill in the blanks. Remember to write the steps in sequence.

(Answers will vary, but students should have been able to summarize each step.)

Giving a Permanent

I. The three steps before waving:

A. _____
   _____

B. _____
   _____

C. _____
   _____

II. The steps to follow in waving:

A. _____

B. _____

C. _____

III. Testing

IV. The last steps after waving:

A. _____

B. _____

C. _____

● First, select a wave lotion by examining the hair carefully. Is it normal or resistant? Is it limp, soft, and fine? Or is it extra dry and tinted? Each type needs a different lotion.

● When the proper wave lotion has been chosen, the next step is to wash the hair. Use a mild shampoo. Make sure you rinse hair thoroughly. Then dry the hair with a towel.

● How much body and wave the hair gets depends on the sizes of the rods to be used. Select the right rods.

● Waving or processing begins by parting the hair into three sections: 1. the neckline and lower back; 2. the front area, from ear to ear; 3. the crown area. When this is done, apply the lotion about half an inch from the scalp. Start with the area on the neckline. Apply lotion and wind hair one curl at a time. After you've wound all the hair in this section, do the same waving process on the other two sections.

● Take the first test curl immediately. For normal and fine hair, the next tests are done every three minutes. For bleached, tinted, or extra dry hair, test every minute until you get the desired wave.

● Finally, rinse and neutralize the wound curls. First, rinse thoroughly using comfortably hot water, for three minutes. Without removing the rods, blot each curl with a towel. Next, apply the neutralizer to each curl from top to bottom. Repeat the application to top of curls. Wait for five minutes before removing the rods. Apply the remaining neutralizer to curls and gently massage the hair with the palms of hands. The last step to a good wave is a thorough rinsing with warm water and towel drying.

Travel Agent

Writing Specific Information

When will the plane leave? Which airport will it leave from? What is the flight number? What kind of plane is it? How much is the fare? How much baggage is allowed?

These are just some of the questions frequently asked a travel agent. It is essential to be accurate and specific in giving answers or information. Any error, any detail left out, may confuse and irritate a customer.

Writing brief, but clear and accurate sentences is a skill you will find useful.

Tips on Giving Information

● Double-check any doubtful information with another source. For example, always verify a fare listed on a schedule. Airfares are always subject to change. Call the airline. Make sure the fare is still valid.

● Be as detailed as you possibly can. Include as many W's (who, what, when, where, why) as necessary. "TWA flight 202 leaves Chicago from O'Hare airport at 12 noon" is more specific than: "The plane leaves Chicago at 12."

● When asked about time, always identify a.m. or p.m.

● Always write information in complete sentences.

Words to Know

Brochure — a small pamphlet

Schedule — a list of fares and/or a timetable

Specific — detailed

Transfers — transportation to and from airports

Verify — to make sure

1. Brochures are common sources of information for travel agents. Read this one. What is a "B ML"?

Breakfast meal

A *MEXICO CITY, TAXCO AND ACAPULCO. $129-$340* PLUS AIRFARE.*
Make the most of your time by dividing it among these three famous and exciting cities. Stay at selected hotels for 3 nights in Mexico City, 1 night in Taxco, and 3 nights in Acapulco. Your transfers are included. And so is a tour of Mexico City and the Pyramids.

B *MEXICO CITY. $77-$235* PLUS AIRFARE.*
Endless attractions are waiting for you in this beautiful city of contrasts. Enjoy 8 days/7 nights at your choice of selected hotels. And you'll get a sight-seeing tour of Mexico City. Round-trip airport transfers are included.

From Chicago/O'Hare to Mexico City

Freq*	Airline/Code	Flight #	Leaves	Arrives	EQ*	ML*
1, 3	American/AA	057	9:05AM	1:06PM	DC10	B
2, 4	Mexicana/MX	803	8:45AM	1:40PM	727	—
5, 6	Braniff/BN	147	3:05PM	8:45PM	747	SD

From Mexico City to Chicago/O'Hare

Freq*	Airline/Code	Flight #	Leaves	Arrives	EQ*	ML*
2, 7	American/AA	104	10:55AM	2:37PM	DC10	L
1, 3	Mexicana/MX	800	9:50AM	1:30PM	727	B
4, 5	Braniff/BN	052	2:15PM	5:57PM	747	L

Sample round-trip airfares
First Class: $412.00
Economy: $320.00

*Freq — days operating
(1 — Mon., 2 — Tues.)
*EQ — kind of plane
*ML — meal served

2. Improve the sentences at the right. Make the italicized words more specific. Add details found in the brochure on page 76. Rewrite the sentences on the lines provided.

a. *The plane* from Chicago arrives in Mexico *at around 1:00.*

_____

_____

b. *One week* in Mexico will cost *$77 plus airfare.*

_____

_____

c. *Mexicana* leaves from Chicago *twice a week.*

_____

_____

3. Suppose you are a travel agent in Chicago. What information will you give the passengers at the right? Answer their questions in complete sentences.

a. Mr. Wayne Blackstone: "What is my schedule if I leave on a Monday?"

_____

_____

b. Ms. Carina Lopez: "How long will I stay in each of the three cities in Mexico?"

_____

_____

4. Mr. and Mrs. Jackson want to leave on a Saturday and return the next Sunday. They want to see three cities in Mexico. Give them the details of their trip. The paragraph has been started for you.

At 3:05 p.m. on Saturday, you will board Braniff flight number 147 at the O'Hare airport.

_____

_____

_____

_____

_____

_____

_____

_____

_____

(Students' wordings for answers to each of the four exercises on this page will vary. However, check spelling, sentence construction, and accuracy of specific details.)

77

Vocabulary Review

1. Spot spelling errors in each of the following signs. Write the correct spelling on the given line.

SCHOOL CROSING 1 KM AHEAD

a. *Crossing*

STATE BOUNDRY One Mile Ahead

b. *Boundary*

LEFT LANE ENDS Merj Right

c. *Merge*

HOSPITEL EMERGENCY Services — to the Left

d. *Hospital*

PARKING For Goverment Officials Only

e. *Government*

2. Who is more likely to say the sentence? Write the person's job on the line. Then underline the word or words that give the clue. If you need help, look back at the Words to Know sections of this unit.

a. "Our special for today is veal goulash."

Food Server

b. "Be at the airport at least 45 minutes before departure."

Travel Agent

c. "The rods may be removed after applying the neutralizer."

Hair Stylist

d. "The causes of an injury can tell you what the effects are."

Home Health Aide

e. "Route 11 is slower because of a detour near Stamford."

Gas Station Attendant

Reading Skills Review

1. What does each sign or symbol mean? Write your answer on the line.

a. _No U-turn_

b. _Two-way traffic_

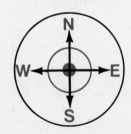

c. _Compass rose_

d. _Interstate highway_

2. Are the drivers obeying the signs? Answer YES or NO on the line next to the symbol.

a. A truck driver uses a road that has this sign:

_No_

b. The chauffeur does not stop, look, or listen upon seeing this sign:

_No_

3. The categories included in the menu at Stella's Coffee Shop are: *Appetizers, Soup, Entrees, Desserts,* and *Beverages.* Under what category can you find the following items?

a. Roast Duck _____ _Entrees_

b. Clam Chowder _____ _Soups_

c. Sweet Roll _____ _Desserts_

d. Lemonade _____ _Beverages_

4. Underline the cause and circle the effect in each of these statements.

a. Brian Peters is the (last to be hired) because he's a high school dropout.

b. New machines will (open up new kinds of jobs.)

Writing Skills Review

1. Rewrite this set of directions in outline form.

People who work in a very hot place can suffer from heat cramps. When it happens, they will need first aid. First, look for symptoms such as muscle cramps in the legs and stomach, too much sweating, and faintness. Next, apply first aid. Move the victim to a cool place and give him or her sips of salted drinking water (one teaspoon of salt to one quart of water). Then, press the cramped muscle with your hand.

Title: _____ *First Aid for Heat Cramps* _____

I. _____ *Symptoms* _____

  A. _____ *Muscle cramps* _____

  B. _____ *Sweating* _____

  C. _____ *Faintness* _____

II. _____ *Treatment* _____

  A. _____ *Move to cool Place* _____

  B. _____ *Give sips of salted water* _____

  C. _____ *Press cramped muscle.* _____

2. Which sentence is better? Put a check inside the box next to each sentence that gives clear information.

a. ☐ Take a train, get off when it stops, and walk straight.

☑ Take the uptown train, get off at 59th, and walk north.

b. ☑ Meet me at the corner of Market and Post at 6:00 p.m.

☐ I will meet you around the corner at around 6:00.

c. ☐ I would like to order a meal.

☑ I would like to order pot roast with baked potatoes and green salad.

3. Improve the following sentences. Make the italicized words more specific. First, think of all the necessary information that you must include in each sentence. Then write your sentence on the lines.

a. *The bus* leaves *the station* at 3:00.

_____

_____

_____

b. Use *the highway* to the *third exit* and make a *turn* on the *street*.

_____

_____

_____

(Answers will vary, but check sentences for specific information given. They should be as detailed as possible.)

Unit 6

Working with Your Hands

You can turn your knack for fixing things into cash. Many businesses hire apprentices — inexperienced employees who are trained on the job for a specialized trade. Generally, the only requirements for such a position are a willingness to learn and some basic skills. If you've repaired toasters and alarm clocks around the house, assembled a tricycle for a younger brother or sister, or made a pair of slacks from a pattern, you can use this knowledge to land a full- or part-time job.

Oil or Gas Burner Mechanic

Reading Diagrams

As long as we heat homes with oil or gas, there will be a need for oil or gas burner mechanics. These men and women must be thoroughly familiar with the burner's various parts and how these parts work together.

Oil and gas burners are complex machines. Very often, the mechanic finds it necessary to use diagrams.

Words to Know

Combustion — the burning process

Diagram — a line drawing of an object that shows its parts and/or how it works

Nozzle — a small spout

Tips

What Diagrams Can Show

● **Connections** — where something is attached to. Look for the oil supply line in the diagram. Notice that it leads to the oil pump.

● **Relative sizes of parts** — Some parts are smaller or bigger than others. Notice how the diagram shows the thickness of the walls of the combustion chamber.

● **How something works** — The master switch in the diagram shows that the burner can be turned on and off.

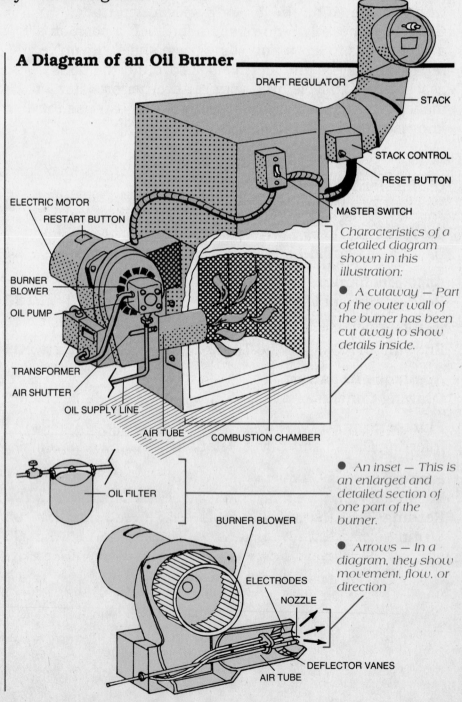

A Diagram of an Oil Burner

DRAFT REGULATOR

STACK

STACK CONTROL

RESET BUTTON

MASTER SWITCH

ELECTRIC MOTOR

RESTART BUTTON

BURNER BLOWER

OIL PUMP

TRANSFORMER

AIR SHUTTER

OIL SUPPLY LINE

AIR TUBE

COMBUSTION CHAMBER

OIL FILTER

BURNER BLOWER

ELECTRODES

NOZZLE

DEFLECTOR VANES

AIR TUBE

Characteristics of a detailed diagram shown in this illustration:

● *A cutaway — Part of the outer wall of the burner has been cut away to show details inside.*

● *An inset — This is an enlarged and detailed section of one part of the burner.*

● *Arrows — In a diagram, they show movement, flow, or direction*

1. Study the diagram on the opposite page very carefully. Underline the word or phrase that correctly completes each sentence.

a. Air flows through the air tube into the

nozzle.   blower.   <u>combustion chamber.</u>

b. The oil supply line does not run through the

<u>stack.</u>   oil pump.   air shutter.

c. The motor is directly attached to the

<u>blower.</u>   air tube.   transformer.

d. Air and oil meet in the

air tube.   oil line.   <u>combustion chamber.</u>

e. The reset button is found on the
motor.   <u>stack control.</u>   draft regulator.

2. Study the diagram once more. Then read each of the following statements. If the statement is true, write T on the given line. If the statement is false, write F.

__F__ **a.** Air in the air tube flows in a clockwise direction.

__T__ **b.** When the master switch is turned off, the motor stops.

__F__ **c.** Oil passes through the oil filter and the oil pump after it goes through the air tube.

__F__ **d.** The electrodes run through the oil line.

__T__ **e.** If the blower stops, the air will not circulate.

__F__ **f.** To restart the blower, flip the master switch.

__T__ **g.** Oil will not reach the combustion chamber if the nozzle is clogged.

__T__ **h.** The stack provides an exit for gases from the combustion chamber.

__F__ **i.** Oil will not get as far as the air tube if the stack control is not functioning.

__T__ **j.** Oil will not reach the combustion chamber if the oil filter is clogged.

Garment Worker

Using a Pattern

There are dozens of jobs available in the clothing field — from retail selling in a fabric store, to manufacturing, to custom tailoring. Your basic knowledge of how a garment is put together is vital, whether you are a tailor, a dressmaker, or a sewing machine operator.

Words to Know

Baste —to sew with long, loose stitches

Bias — a line diagonal to the grain of a fabric

Grain — the direction in which the fibers of a piece of cloth are arranged.

Selvage — the finished edge of a fabric that prevents threads from disengaging

View A, B, C, etc. — the variations in style that can be made with one pattern

Vital — very important, or very necessary

The pattern is another form of diagram.

A clothing pattern is a diagram that has been divided into several pieces. All of the pieces fit together to form the garment.

The Key to the Symbols

The instructions that come with the pattern have a key to the symbols used on the pattern pieces. The key gives the meaning of each symbol.

Grainline: This line is placed on the fabric parallel to the grain.

Fold: The arrows are placed on the folded edge of the fabric. The fabric is folded in half before laying out the pattern. Two of every piece of the pattern is cut unless otherwise indicated.

Cutting line: The piece is cut along this line.

Notches: When pieces are pinned before basting, notches must line up.

Transfer markings: Transfer these markings to the fabric using tailor's chalk, thread, or a tracing wheel.

Seam line: Usually 5/8" (15 mm.) from the edge of the pattern piece. Unless otherwise indicated, this is also the stitching line.

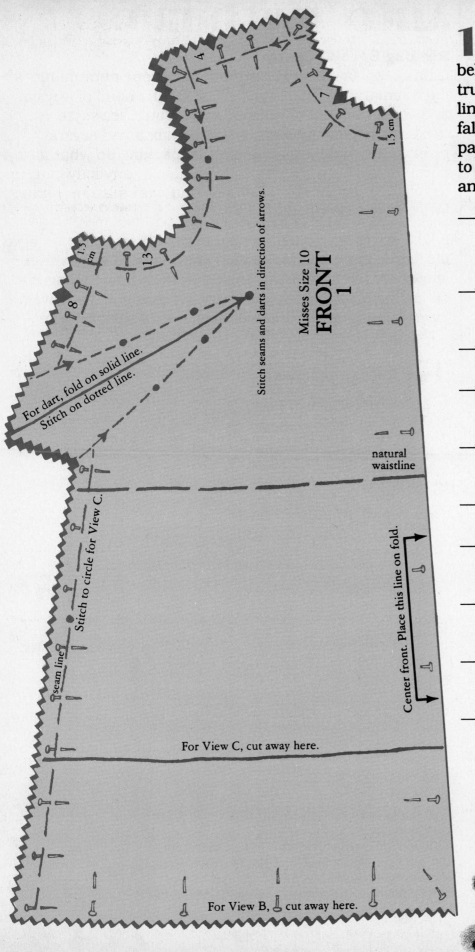

For dart, fold on solid line.
Stitch on dotted line.

Stitch seams and darts in direction of arrows.

1.5 cm

1.5 cm

4

7

8

13

Misses Size 10
FRONT
1

natural waistline

Stitch to circle for View C.

seam line

Center front. Place this line on fold.

For View C, cut away here.

For View B, cut away here.

1. Read each statement below. If the statement is true, write T on the given line. If the statement is false, write F. Use the pattern piece on this page to help you give the correct answer.

__T__ **a.** The pattern piece shown on this page is to be placed on the folded edge of the fabric.

__F__ **b.** After cutting, the two front pieces will have to be sewn together.

__F__ **c.** The piece is cut along the broken line.

__F__ **d.** The dart is stitched from the point of the triangle downward.

__F__ **e.** The dress shown in View C is longer than the one shown in View B.

__F__ **f.** The pattern shown is for a junior size garment.

__T__ **g.** The shoulder is stitched from the neck edge to the armhole edge.

__F__ **h.** For View B, the side seam is stitched to the circle.

__T__ **i.** When stitching seams, follow the direction of the arrows.

__F__ **j.** When stitching darts, follow the solid line.

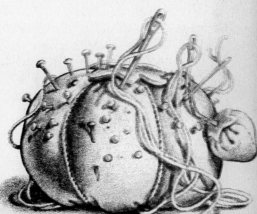

Auto Mechanic

Reading Special Charts

It has been said that the automobile is one of humanity's most remarkable machines. Just lift the hood of any car and you'll see a lot of reasons why. You'll see some *doohickies*, a few *whatzis*, a *thingamabob* and several *gizmos* that make this remarkable machine do what it does. And with some basic skills, almost anybody can translate a *gizmo* into a radiator that works and a *whatzit* into a horn that blows.

Like a driver who must be able to read road maps, an auto mechanic must be able to read some special charts that show how the parts of an engine work or how to diagnose an engine problem. A flow chart, for example, can give a clear, step-by-step outline of how to fix a car problem.

Words to Know

Diagnose — to investigate the cause of a problem

Hood — movable metal covering over a car's engine

Mechanic — a person who repairs machines

Outcome — the result of a series of related events

Tips on Flow Charts

- Each step is written in a box.
- One box is connected to another box by a line.
- A flow chart is read from top to bottom (see chart below), from left to right.
- Simple flow charts have a few steps. Complex ones have several steps.

This is part of a flow chart.

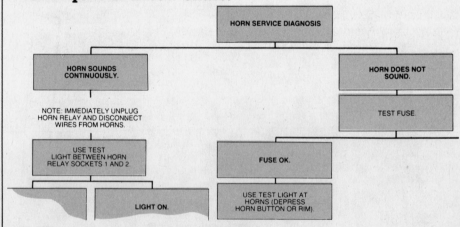

According to the horn service chart above:

- A faulty horn doesn't sound at all or it sounds continuously.
- If you follow the direction of the chart from a box that states the problem, the next box along the way will tell you what to do.
- The following boxes will give you the possible outcomes.

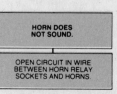

Study the complete flow chart for the car horn service diagnosis.

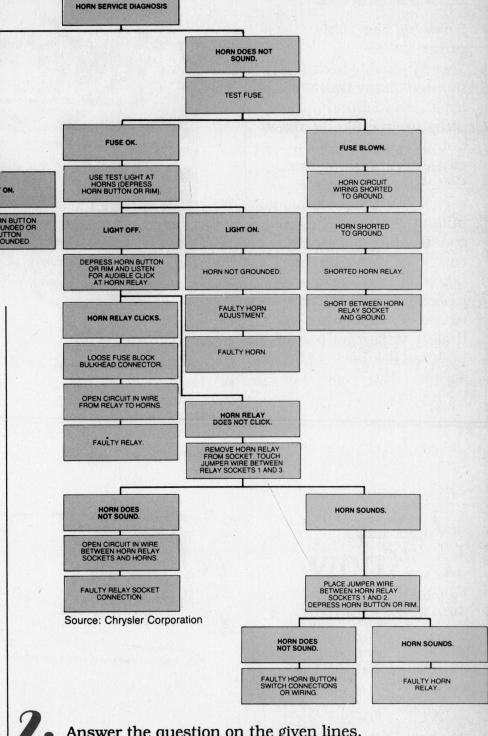

Source: Chrysler Corporation

1. Circle the word or phrase that answers the question correctly.

a. In what direction should the flow chart be followed?

left to right

(top to bottom)

right to left

b. What is given in the boxes with darker letters?

warnings

directions

(possible outcomes)

c. According to the chart, what is the first thing to do if the horn does not sound?

(Test fuse.)

Test light.

Unplug relay.

d. How many different things might have caused a blown fuse?

two

(four)

six

2. Answer the question on the given lines.

Mr. Milton's car horn does not sound at all. You checked the fuse, and it's OK. You used the test light, and it remained on. What are three possible causes of Mr. Milton's problem?

horn not grounded

faulty horn adjustment

faulty horn

87

Builder

Knowing the Tools of the Trade

We've probably been builders many times in our lives. We've found pleasure in building towers out of alphabet blocks, castles out of sand, and three-story houses out of cards. For the professional builder, the pleasures of constructing something can be as varied as the many different tools and materials he or she has to use. A builder knows that an important part of building is knowing and selecting the proper tool for a particular job.

Words to Know

Portable — can be easily carried

Threads — the coiling pattern on a screw that allows it to be driven into a thick building material

Comparisons and Contrasts

● When you compare two or more things, you notice their similarities.

● When you contrast two or more things, you are looking specifically for their differences.

Look at these tools:

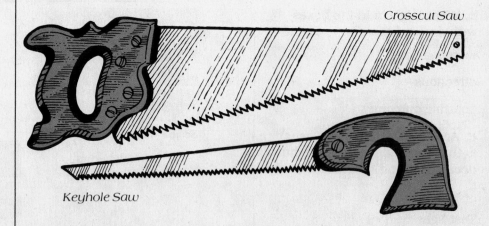

Crosscut Saw

Keyhole Saw

How are these tools similar?

- Both are saws.
- Both have one cutting edge.
- Both have grip handles.
- Both are portable.
- Both have tapered blades.

How are these tools different?

- Crosscut saw is larger in length and width.
- Keyhole saw has a slanted nose.
- Crosscut saw blade has wider teeth.
- Keyhole saw has pistol grip.

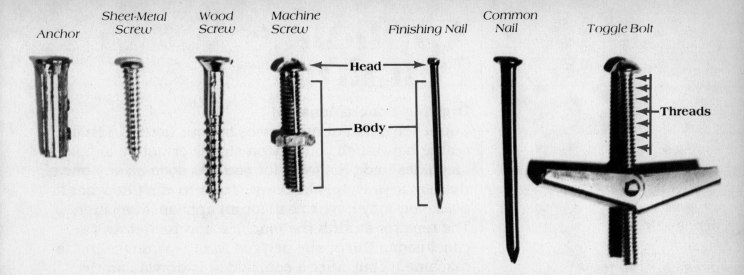

Anchor   Sheet-Metal Screw   Wood Screw   Machine Screw   Finishing Nail   Common Nail   Toggle Bolt

Head — Body — Threads

1. Study the fasteners shown above. Then read the following questions and the answers given. Cross out the incorrect answers.

a. Which fasteners have similar heads?
- toggle bolt
- ~~finishing nail~~
- machine screw

b. In what ways are the heads of the seven fasteners different?
- different sizes
- different shapes
- ~~different names~~

c. How is the finishing nail similar to the common nail?
- ~~same size head~~
- similar pointed tip
- similar body shape

d. How is the body of the wood screw different from the body of the sheet-metal screw?
- Top part of the body has no threads.
- ~~It has bigger heads.~~

2. Read the example given below. Then complete the last two statements. Write your answers on the given lines. Refer to the illustration of fasteners to help you answer correctly.

Here's an example of how you draw a conclusion:

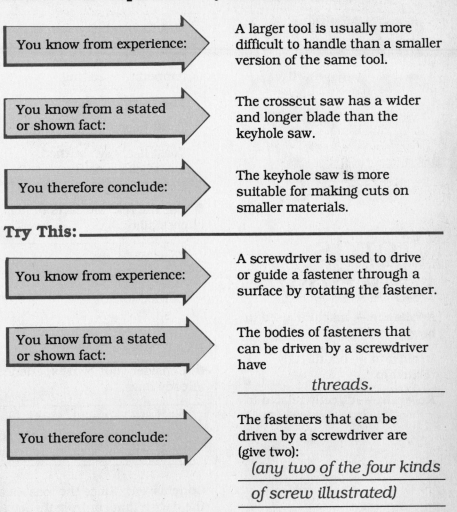

You know from experience: A larger tool is usually more difficult to handle than a smaller version of the same tool.

You know from a stated or shown fact: The crosscut saw has a wider and longer blade than the keyhole saw.

You therefore conclude: The keyhole saw is more suitable for making cuts on smaller materials.

Try This:

You know from experience: A screwdriver is used to drive or guide a fastener through a surface by rotating the fastener.

You know from a stated or shown fact: The bodies of fasteners that can be driven by a screwdriver have

threads.

You therefore conclude: The fasteners that can be driven by a screwdriver are (give two):
(any two of the four kinds

of screw illustrated)

Appliance Repairer

Drawing Conclusions

Count the different appliances in your house. You'll realize how much you rely on simple or not-so-simple machines to do the work for you. As soon as any one of these machines breaks down, and you can't do what it does, you may have to call for an appliance repairer. The repairer studies the machine and then draws a conclusion. (He or she decides what is wrong with the machine.) Only after a conclusion is drawn can the repair be made on the troubled appliance. When the machine works again, you'll appreciate the skilled job the repairer does.

Tips for Drawing a Correct Conclusion

- Consider only the relevant facts.

> Mrs. Dobbs has a four-slice toaster which she bought last year. Recently, the toaster has been popping up, but the toast is always burned. This happens even on the lightest temperature setting.
>
> | The relevant facts: | The irrelevant facts: |
> | --- | --- |
> | Toast pops up. | Four-slice toaster. |
> | Toast is always burned, regardless of setting. | Toaster purchased last year. |

- Use the relevant facts to help you narrow down the field of possibility.

> | | |
> | --- | --- |
> | Toast pops up. | If it pops up, it isn't the spring mechanism. |
> | Burned toast. | If it is heating, it isn't the wiring or electrical connections. |

- Consider your own experiences and the knowledge that you already have.

> The temperature setting on a toaster controls the amount of time the heat will reach the toast. The darker the setting, the longer the toast needs to be heated.

Conclusion: Since the toast is always burned, the problem lies in the device that controls the length of time the heat reaches the toast.

Words to Know

Appliance — machine used in homes or offices

Irrelevant — not directly related to

Relevant — directly related to

Read each paragraph carefully. Then answer each question on the given lines.

1. Ms. Gleason has a 48-hour wind-up alarm clock. There are two keys: one winds the main clock spring and the other, winds the spring for the alarm. A setting knob turns a pointer that indicates what time the alarm will go off. The alarm rings for as long as it takes the spring to unwind. Ms. Gleason's clock runs well, but the alarm does not ring.

a. Why couldn't the problem be in the main clock spring?
The main clock spring has nothing to do

with the alarm.

b. Why could the problem be in the alarm spring?
She must wind the alarm spring before

the alarm can go off.

c. Why could the problem be in the alarm-setting knob?
The alarm setting knob may not be in the proper

position so that the alarm is not actually set.

2. Mr. Harbro's electric razor does not work continuously. It keeps starting and stopping. There is nothing wrong with Mr. Harbro's electrical outlet, and the razor does not have an on/off switch.

a. How do you know that the razor is not getting a constant flow of electricity?
It keeps starting and stopping.

b. Why couldn't the problem be in the on/off switch?
It doesn't have one.

c. Why could the problem be in the razor's electric cord?
There might be a short in the cord.

d. Why could the problem be in the motor?
The motor may be overheating.

Plumber

Inferring Cause and Effect Relationships

Suppose you, as the plumber, are called to the Fenway residence. You are asked to fix the kitchen faucet. When you get there, do you immediately take out all your tools and get the job done? Not so quick, plumber. Like all people who have to do repairs, a plumber must first identify the problem, its effect, and its cause.

Words to Know

Disassemble — take apart

Dismantle — take apart

Event — something that happens

Reassemble — put together

Valve — structure that opens and closes to control the flow of liquids or gases

Cause and Effect

● If you turn the faucet on (cause), pressure is released from the valve (effect).
● When pressure is released from the valve (cause), water flows through the faucet (effect).

Therefore:
● Cause (turning the faucet on) is the reason why an event (pressure is released from the valve) occurs.
● Effect (pressure is released from the valve) is the event brought about by a particular action (turning the faucet on).

Sometimes an event can have more than one cause, for example, a leaking faucet (event or effect):

Possible cause:

worn washer

packing is too loose

valve is not working

seat is worn

A SIMPLE PLUMBING REPAIR

Dripping faucets are the most common plumbing problem. Normally a new washer is all that is required. If water leaks around the stem, the packing is either loose or needs replacing. To repair the faucet, first shut off the water at the shutoff valve nearest the particular faucet.

Disassemble the faucet by removing the handle, packing nut, packing, and stem in that order. You may have to set the handle back on the stem and use it to unscrew and remove the stem.

Remove the screw and worn washer from the stem. Clean the washer cup and install a new washer of the proper size and type.

Reassemble the faucet. Handles of mixing faucets should be in matched positions.

1. Read this article with the diagram of a faucet. Then answer questions **a** and **b**. Write your answers on the given lines.

a. If a faucet leaks or drips, what's probably needed? *(any of these possible answers is correct: a new washer; a new seat; tighten packing; repair valve)*

b. What's the first thing to do when repairing a leaking faucet? *Shut off the water at the nearest shut off valve.*

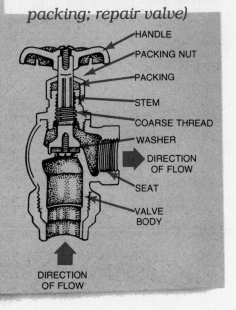

HANDLE
PACKING NUT
PACKING
STEM
COARSE THREAD
WASHER
DIRECTION OF FLOW
SEAT
VALVE BODY
DIRECTION OF FLOW

2. Choose the correct words from the list given in parentheses and write them on the lines.

Take the faucet apart by removing parts in this order:

(seat, stem, valve, packing, handle, packing nut)

a. *handle*
b. *packing nut*
c. *packing*
d. *stem*

3. Decide what each question or answer has — a cause or an effect. To complete each statement, write CAUSE or EFFECT on the given line.

Questions:

a. If I dismantle the faucet, what will happen?

Taking apart the faucet is the
cause .

b. If pressure is released, what will happen?

Released pressure is the
cause .

c. How do I stop the flow of water?

Water stopped flowing is the
effect .

Answers:

a. Pressure will be released on the valve.

Released pressure is the
effect .

b. The water will flow out.

Water flowing out is the
effect .

c. Shut off the water at the shutoff valve (under the sink.)

Shutting off the water is the
cause .

93

Vocabulary Review

1. Synonyms are words that have almost the same meaning. Underline the synonym for each word in dark type in rows a, b, c, d, and e.

a. **repair**	<u>fix</u>	disassemble	baste
b. **diagram**	faucet	selvage	<u>drawing</u>
c. **combustion**	machine	<u>burning</u>	connection
d. **garment**	grain	bias	<u>clothing</u>
e. **diagnose**	outcome	<u>examine</u>	nozzle

2. Antonyms are words that have opposite meanings. Underline the antonym of the italicized word.

a. The plumber *dismantled* the faucet.

<u>reassembled</u>   repaired   disassembled

b. The oil burner is a highly *complex* machine.

complicated   <u>simple</u>   pattern

c. A worn washer may be the *cause* of a leaking faucet.

reason   cure   <u>effect</u>

d. Conclusions should be based on *relevant* facts.

<u>irrelevant</u>   related   repairable

e. The builder uses *portable* tools.

<u>immobile</u>   movable   small

3. Prefixes and suffixes are clues to the meaning of words. Study the underlined prefix or suffix of each word. Then complete the meaning of the word.

a. <u>re</u>assemble: put together _____ *again* _____

b. repair<u>er</u>: _____ *person who* _____ fixes things

c. <u>un</u>familiar: _____ *not* _____ known

d. cause<u>less</u>: _____ *without* _____ a cause

94

Reading Skills Review

1. Read this illustrated set of directions on how to use a hammer. Then answer the following questions in complete sentences.

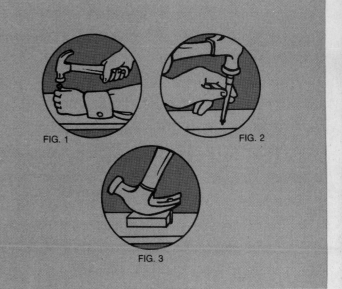

HOW TO USE A CLAW HAMMER

• Hold the hammer, head down, near the end of the handle for more hitting power. First, hold a nail in place and tap it gently with the hammer head until it is firmly set. Then hit the nail straight in. (See Fig. 1)

• Use a nail set (Fig. 2) to avoid hammer marks on the wood. You can also use another nail to drive a nail the last one-eighth inch into the wood.

• Use the claw end of the hammer to remove a nail. To avoid marking the wood, place a small block of wood under the hammer head. (Fig. 3)

FIG. 1   FIG. 2   FIG. 3

a. What is the effect of holding a hammer near the end of the handle?

The hammer will have more hitting power.

b. Why should you use a nail set?

A nail set is used to avoid hammer marks on the wood.

c. What is the purpose of the claw end of the hammer?

The claw end is used to remove a nail.

2. Now look at these illustrations showing the uses of slip joint pliers. Then read each conclusion that follows. Write T on the line if the conclusion is true. Write F if it is false.

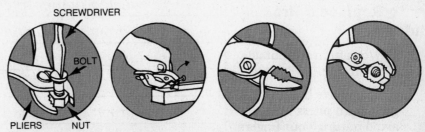

SCREWDRIVER
BOLT
PLIERS   NUT

_T_ **a.** Pliers can hold a nut while you turn a bolt with a screwdriver.

_F_ **b.** Pliers should not be used for straightening bent nails.

_T_ **c.** Pliers can be used to bend or cut wire.

_F_ **d.** Never use pliers for turning nuts.

Writing Skills Review

1. Write step-by-step directions describing the illustrated flow chart at the right. Remember to write in complete sentences.

First Step: _____
_____

Second Step: _____
_____

Last Step: _____
_____

(Students' wordings for answers will vary. Check for correctness in sentence structure and sequence of steps.)

HOW TO SET FLEXIBLE TILES

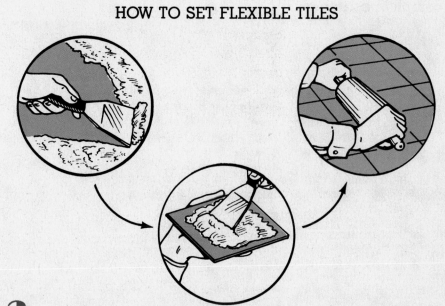

2. Which of the following groups of words in **a, b, c, d,** and **e** are complete sentences (with subject and predicate)? Write **S** on the line for each complete sentence. Write **F** on the line for each fragment.

How to Replace a Broken Window

__S__ **a.** Work from the outside of the frame.

__F__ **b.** To remove broken glass with pliers and avoid cutting your fingers.

__F__ **c.** Old putty removed.

__S__ **d.** Place a thin ribbon of putty in the frame.

__F__ **e.** New glass firmly placed against the putty.

3. Now rewrite the directions in Exercise 2 in paragraph form. Remember to make all fragments into complete sentences.

(Students' wordings for answers will vary.
Check for correctness in sentence structure
and sequence of steps.)
Suggested paragraph:
Work from the outside of the frame. Remove
broken glass with pliers to avoid cutting your
fingers. Remove old putty. Place a thin ribbon
of putty in the frame. Place new glass firmly
against the putty.
_____
_____
_____

Unit 7

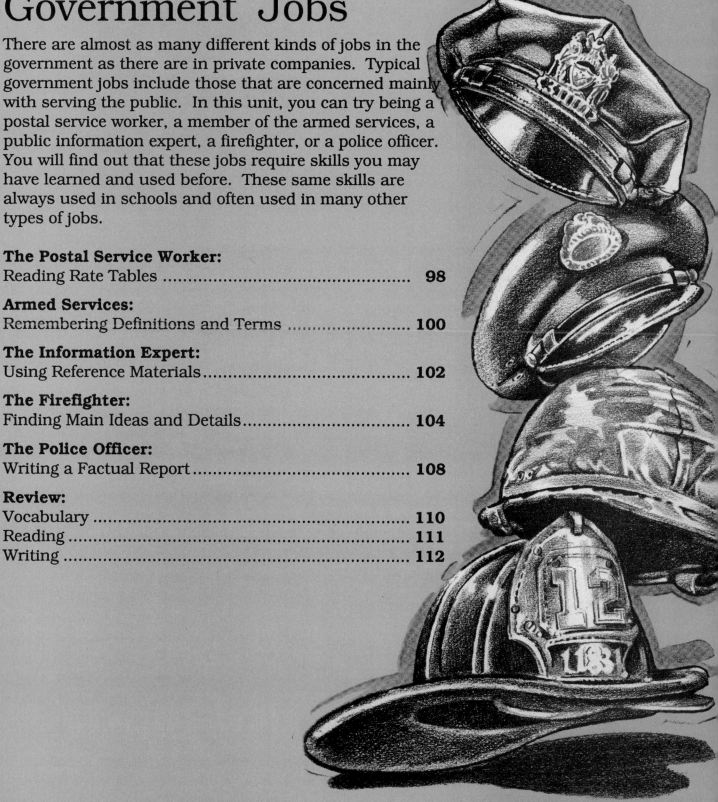

Government Jobs

There are almost as many different kinds of jobs in the government as there are in private companies. Typical government jobs include those that are concerned mainly with serving the public. In this unit, you can try being a postal service worker, a member of the armed services, a public information expert, a firefighter, or a police officer. You will find out that these jobs require skills you may have learned and used before. These same skills are always used in schools and often used in many other types of jobs.

The Postal Service Worker

Reading Rate Tables

Working in the Post Office could mean weighing mail, calculating rates, selling stamps, sorting mail, or making deliveries. Whatever the task, careful reading is essential.

DOMESTIC MAIL: FIRST CLASS

Letter Rates

1st ounce	25 ¢
Each add'l ounce	20 ¢
Over 12 ounces	Priority mail (heavy pieces) rates apply.

Single postal cards sold by the Post Office .... 15 ¢ each

Double postal cards sold by the Post Office .... 30 ¢ each half

Single postcards .... 15 ¢ each

Double postcards (Reply half of double postcard does not have to bear postage when originally mailed.) .... 15 ¢ each half

DOMESTIC MAIL: THIRD CLASS

Circulars, books, catalogs, and other printed matter, merchandise, seeds, cuttings, bulbs, roots, scions, and plants, weighing less than 16 ounces.

SINGLE PIECE RATE

1 oz	$0.25	8 oz	$1.10
2 oz	0.45	10 oz	1.20
3 oz	0.65	12 oz	1.30
4 oz	0.85	14 oz	1.40
6 oz	1.00	Over 14 oz	1.50

INTERNATIONAL MAIL: LETTERS

Air Rates   *MAXIMUM WEIGHT: 4 LBS.*

1. All countries except those listed in 2.

45 cents per HALF ounce through 2 ounces.

45 cents each additional HALF ounce or fraction.

2. Central America, Colombia, Venezuela, Caribbean Islands, Bahamas, Bermuda, St. Pierre and Miquelon. Also from American Samoa to Western Samoa and from Guam to the Philippines.

25 cents per HALF ounce through 2 ounces

21 cents each additional HALF ounce or fraction

Words to Know

Airmail — sent by airplane

Domestic — within the U. S.

First Class — the usual way letters and postcards are sent

International — to a foreign country

Table — information condensed in list form

Third class — the usual way printed matter is sent; costs less than first class

A Quick Look at Rate Tables

Rate tables are used by window clerks to help calculate postage charges for customers. Study these tables for first- and third-class mail. The columns describe the type of mail and the rate for each piece of mail.

Use the postal rate tables on the opposite page to do the following exercises.

1. Suppose you are the information clerk at the Post Office. How would you answer the following questions from customers?

a. Which is cheaper — first class or third class?
over 4 ounces — third class is cheaper

b. How heavy can each piece of first-class mail be?
up to 12 ounces

c. What is the difference in cost between a single postcard and a double postcard?
15¢

d. Is it possible to send a plant to San Francisco by mail? If so, how?
Yes, by third class mail

e. Will these two letters have the same amount of postage? One goes to the Philippines and the other goes to Colombia.
Yes, if the letter to the Philippines comes from Guam.

If not, amount of postage will be different.

2. Calculate the cost of postage for each piece of mail described in the chart.

Description	Weight	Destination	Cost of Postage
bag of seeds	5 oz.	Maryland	$ 0.85
letter	1 oz.	France	0.90
postcard	1/4 oz.	Texas	0.15
letter	1/2 oz.	Bermuda	0.25
letter	3 oz.	Wyoming	0.65

3. How much change would you give to each customer described below?

a. Mr. Sands, who gives you a $5 bill for 15 single postcards.
$ 2.75

b. Mrs. Tophan, who gives you a $10 bill to pay for three separate catalogs: one weighs 8 oz., one weighs 14 oz., and one weighs 14.77 oz.
$ 6.00

Armed Services

Remembering Definitions and Terms

More and more, the armed services need skilled people. Even basic training involves reading and remembering rules, codes of conduct, and military terms.

Reading the Military Clock

The armed services use a 24-hour clock to tell time. The clock starts at 0100 (pronounced *o one hundred*) for 1:00 a.m. and ends at 2400 (pronounced *twenty-four hundred*) for 12:00 midnight.

Words to Know

Armed services — army, navy, marines, and air force

Jargon — special vocabulary or idiom used by a particular group

Recruit — a new member of the armed services

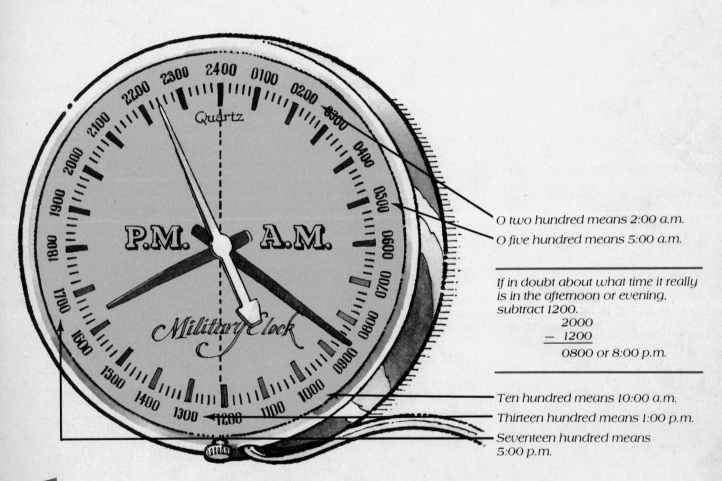

O two hundred means 2:00 a.m.
O five hundred means 5:00 a.m.

If in doubt about what time it really is in the afternoon or evening, subtract 1200.

$$2000$$
$$-\ 1200$$
$$\overline{0800 \text{ or } 8:00 \text{ p.m.}}$$

Ten hundred means 10:00 a.m.
Thirteen hundred means 1:00 p.m.
Seventeen hundred means 5:00 p.m.

1. Give the military term and pronunciation for each of these times.

	Military Term	Pronunciation
a. 3:00 a.m.	0300	o three hundred
b. 11:00 a.m.	1100	eleven hundred
c. 10:00 p.m.	2200	twenty-two hundred
d. 12:00 noon	1200	twelve hundred
e. 3:00 p.m.	1500	fifteen hundred

Military Jargon

● The following terms refer to marching drill.

Cadence — uniform step and rhythm in marching
Double time — cadence at 180 steps per minute
Quick time — cadence at 120 steps per minute; normal rhythm for drills and ceremonies
Slow time — cadence at 60 steps per minute; used for funerals only

● Each of the armed services uses special terms. Marines, for example, learn this new vocabulary for parts of a building or ship.

Below — downstairs
Brightwork — brass or shiny metal
Bulkhead — wall
Bunks — beds
Deck — floor
GI can — trash container
Quarters — a place to live
Topside — upstairs

2. Without looking back, answer these questions. Write your answers on the given lines.

a. Which is the normal drill cadence? _____ *quick time* _____

b. Marines may be ordered to polish the _____ *brightwork* _____.

c. Garbage is thrown in the _____ *GI can* _____.

d. Which is the fastest cadence? _____ *double time* _____

e. When marines are ordered to go below, they go _____ *downstairs* _____.

3. Write the meaning of the following sentences.

a. Scrub the deck. _____ *Mop the floor.* _____

b. Report topside at 1500. _____ *Report upstairs at 3:00 p.m.* _____

c. Put the bunks below at 0700. _____ *Put the beds downstairs* _____ *at 7:00 a.m.* _____

4. How would you say these sentences if you were a marine?

a. I'll be in my home at 6:00 p.m. _____ *I'll be in my quarters at 1800.* _____

b. You'll find the brass upstairs near my bed. _____ *You'll find the brightwork topside near my bunk.* _____

c. March at 180 steps per minute! _____ *Double time!* _____

The Information Expert

Using Reference Materials

Providing information to the public is an important job in almost every government office. When people ask your office for some facts, you — as the information expert — must be able to obtain those facts quickly and accurately.

Which Reference for What Purpose?

Reference	Purpose
Almanac	To find past and up-to-date facts on many subjects, including sports, news events, politics
Atlas	To find maps of countries
Directory	To find addresses, telephone numbers, or location of persons or offices
Encyclopedia	To find general information on all subjects

How do you locate information in these big books?

If the facts are not alphabetically arranged, look at the **index**. Here, for example, is part of the index of an almanac.

Words to Know

Expert — a person who has a special skill

Index — an alphabetical listing of subjects that gives all the page numbers on which the subject is mentioned

Reference — a source of information

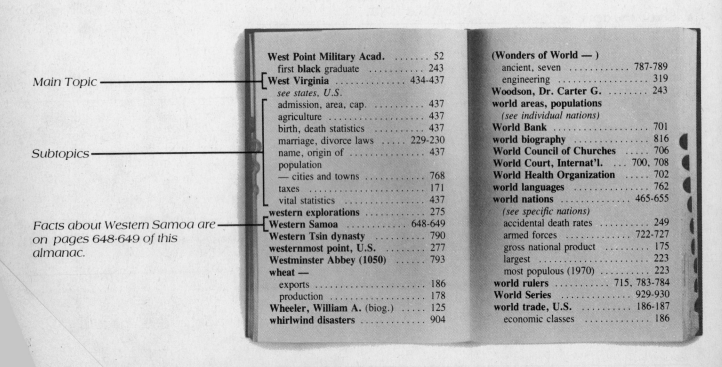

Main Topic

Subtopics

Facts about Western Samoa are on pages 648-649 of this almanac.

West Point Military Acad. 52
  first **black** graduate 243
West Virginia 434-437
  see states, U.S.
  admission, area, cap. 437
  agriculture 437
  birth, death statistics 437
  marriage, divorce laws 229-230
  name, origin of 437
  population
  — cities and towns 768
  taxes 171
  vital statistics 437
western explorations 275
Western Samoa 648-649
Western Tsin dynasty 790
westernmost point, U.S. 277
Westminster Abbey (1050) 793
wheat —
  exports 186
  production 178
Wheeler, William A. (biog.) 125
whirlwind disasters 904

(Wonders of World —)
  ancient, seven 787-789
  engineering 319
Woodson, Dr. Carter G. 243
world areas, populations
  (see individual nations)
World Bank 701
world biography 816
World Council of Churches 706
World Court, Internat'l. ... 700, 708
World Health Organization 702
world languages 762
world nations 465-655
  (see specific nations)
  accidental death rates 249
  armed forces 722-727
  gross national product 175
  largest 223
  most populous (1970) 223
world rulers 715, 783-784
World Series 929-930
world trade, U.S. 186-187
  economic classes 186

1. Here is a list of questions on different topics. Write the name of the reference you would check to find the answer.

a. Who won the Nobel Peace Prize in 1978? _____*almanac*_____

b. Where is Senator Kennedy's office? _____*directory*_____

c. What countries are near Kenya? _____*atlas*_____

d. What is archaeology? _____*encyclopedia*_____

e. Where and how do coconuts grow? _____*encyclopedia*_____

f. What number should I call for job information?
_____*directory*_____

g. Who holds the world record for high jump? _____*almanac*_____

h. What is the shortest highway route between
New York City and Toronto, Canada? _____*atlas*_____

2. Refer to the index on page 102 to answer the following questions.

a. All the topics listed begin with the letter *W.* Why is *World Series* listed before *world trade, U.S.?*
S comes before T in the alphabet.

b. What is listed under the main topics?
subtopics

c. Suppose the main topic *Western Hemisphere* were to be added to this index. Between what topics would it appear?
between western explorations and Western Samoa

3. Write the page or pages you would check to find the answer to each of these questions.

a. How old do people have to be to get married in West Virginia?
pages 229-230

b. What is the most populous nation in the world? *page 223*

c. Who played in the 1979 World Series? _____*pages 929-930*_____

d. How much wheat is exported by the United States?
page 186

The Firefighter

Read this article from a firefighter's pamphlet. It gives you main ideas and details about home fire alarm systems.

A study by the National Fire Protection Association reports that approximately 70 percent of all fire fatalities in the home occur between 11 p.m. and 6 a.m., when most people are sleeping. Ⓐ

The Report of the National Commission on Fire Prevention and Control, entitled *America Burning*, called attention to these facts: about two-thirds of the fire deaths in the United States occur in homes; most people die during the nighttime hours when they are sleeping; most people die from smoke, toxic gases, or lack of oxygen, rather than from heat or the fire itself. The report said, "In countless instances these lives would be saved if the victims were awakened to the presence of fire in its early stages. . . ." As one solution, the report recommends early-warning fire detectors and alarms in homes. Ⓑ

The National Safety Council says that deaths in residential fires could be cut in half through the use of smoke detectors. Ⓐ

There are two types of home fire alarm systems — the heat detector and the smoke detector. The smoke sensitive alarm has won the endorsement of government agencies and fire prevention officials as the more effective lifesaving device. The reason: it reacts much more quickly.

Smoke detectors generally sense the amount of smoke particles in a given area. An abnormal amount triggers an alarm. Ⓑ

Smoke detecting devices can be purchased at hardware and department stores for between $25 and $50.

They come in an assortment of models, including types that can be plugged into wall outlets or wired into a home's electrical system, and others that are battery operated.

In a recent article on smoke detectors, *Consumers Union* concluded, "These devices cost so little and can save so much sorrow that they ought to be the hottest item on the home improvement market." Ⓒ

Ⓐ main idea   **B** details   **C** conclusion

Finding Main Ideas and Details

An important part of a firefighter's job is educating the public about fire prevention. A firefighter usually gets information by reading pamphlets about the latest inventions in fire prevention. Information about things like home fire alarm systems and how they can save lives may be passed along to the public during school or community meetings.

Words to Know

Detectors — equipment that discovers the presence of smoke and gives out a signal or a loud sound

Fatalities — deaths

Prevention — keeping something from happening

Toxic — poisonous

1. Complete these sentences.

a. Most fire fatalities occur when people are ___*sleeping*___ .

b. Most people die from *smoke, toxic gases, or lack of oxygen* .

c. Lives would be saved by using ___*smoke detectors*___ .

d. The reason smoke detectors are more effective than heat detectors is: ___*they react much more quickly*___ .

e. When smoke particles reach the detector, *they trigger an alarm* .

f. Smoke detectors are available at *hardware and department stores* .

g. Smoke detectors cost ___*$25 to $50*___ .

h. Smoke detectors ought to be *the hottest item on the home improvement market* .

2. Write whether each sentence you have completed in exercise 1 is a main idea or a detail.

a. ___*main idea*___

b. ___*detail*___

c. ___*main idea*___

d. ___*detail*___

e. ___*detail*___

f. ___*detail*___

g. ___*detail*___

h. ___*main idea*___

3. What do you think? Which of the three given phrases will best complete the sentence? Put a check mark in the box for your answer.

a. Most fire deaths in the United States occur
- ❑ in big office buildings.
- ❑ in theaters.
- ☑ in homes.

b. Lives would be saved if fire victims
- ❑ slept in the same room.
- ❑ tried to escape by jumping from windows.
- ☑ were awakened to the presence of fire as soon as it started.

c. Smoke detectors
- ❑ will improve homes.
- ☑ must be bought by every homeowner.
- ❑ are hottest when a fire breaks out.

d. A smoke-sensitive alarm is more effective than a heat-sensitive alarm because
- ☑ it reacts quickly.
- ❑ the fire department says so.
- ❑ it makes a louder noise.

The Firefighter

Saying Information in Your Own Words

As a firefighter, you often have to teach the public about preventing fires. The facts that you learn from reading will be more effective if you put them in your own words.

The following is an interview with Mr. Felix Perez, a firefighter.

Note how he has put the facts about home fire alarm systems (see page 104) in his own words.

(see page 104)

WHEN DO MOST FIRE FATALITIES OCCUR?

MANY DEATHS FROM FIRE HAPPEN AT SLEEP TIME, BETWEEN 11 P.M. AND 6 A.M.

WHAT IS THE CAUSE OF MOST FIRE FATALITIES?

A LOT OF PEOPLE DIE BECAUSE THEY BREATHE IN TOO MUCH SMOKE.

WHAT IS A SMOKE DETECTOR?

IT IS AN ALARM THAT WARNS YOU WHEN THERE IS TOO MUCH SMOKE AND, THEREFORE, A FIRE.

WHY WOULD YOU ADVISE EVERY FAMILY TO HAVE ONE IN THEIR HOME?

A SMOKE ALARM CAN SAVE LIVES AND PROPERTY.

Words to Know

Emergency — something that needs immediate action

Escape — to get away

Route — selected way

Tips

for Stating Facts

Facts are remembered better if you state them:
● **clearly** — Use words that your audience will understand.
● **briefly** — Make your statements brief and to the point.

1. Suppose you are a firefighter giving facts about making an escape plan in case of fire. Read the information at the right. Then, in your own words, answer the questions.

a. Why should a family have an escape plan?

to keep family from

panicking and to save

lives when seconds count

_____

_____

b. Is it better to sleep with a bedroom door open or closed? Why?

closed — so that it may

keep smoke out long

enough for you to escape

through a window

_____

c. What is one very important rule to stress?

Once out, stay out till

the fire is out.

_____

_____

_____

MAP OUT AN ESCAPE PLAN

A PLAN CAN BE A LIFESAVER A well-thought-out plan for escaping from every room in your house, particularly the bedrooms, may keep the family from panicking and save lives when seconds count. A bad fire does not burn inch by inch. It can leap through the house, quickly creating temperatures of 800 to 1000 degrees. In such heat, areas far from the original fire can burst into flame.

MARK ESCAPE ROUTES ON PAPER Emergency escape routes are important because fire and smoke spread along the same passages that you normally would use, blocking halls and stairways. Make a rough floor plan, marking possible escape routes — the normal route and an emergency route out of every room, especially out of bedrooms. Is there a porch or garage roof to use as an emergency exit out of the upper story windows? (If you sleep with the bedroom door closed, it could keep smoke out long enough for you to escape through a window.) Consider having rope or chain ladders in upstairs rooms.

DISCUSS THE PLAN Hold a Family Fire Control Meeting, go over the plan, ask for suggestions. Assign somebody to help the very young or old members of the household in escaping. Agree on a place outside to meet and "count noses" to be sure all are out. Emphasize an important rule: once out, stay out until the fire is out.

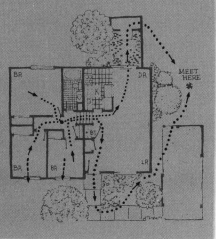

2. After speaking before a community group on the subject "How Fire Victims Can Help Themselves," you, as a firefighter, are asked to give your opinion about what to do in given situations.

a. What should a person who lives in an upper floor do during a fire? Jump? Or stay until the firemen get there?

Your opinion: _(Students' wordings for answers to **a, b, c,**_ _and **d** will vary. Check for correct spelling and grammar.)_

b. Who will a firefighter save first? An invalid, a baby, or a rare bird?

Your opinion: _____

_____

c. What should an oversized person do if trapped in a basement with windows which are not big enough to escape through?

Your opinion: _____

_____

d. You've said: "Once out, stay out until the fire is out." But once out, I realize that my children are still in the house. No firefighter has come to the rescue yet. What should I do in this situation?

Your opinion: _____

_____

The Police Officer

Writing a Factual Report

A major on-the-job activity of police officers is to collect facts about a case. These facts are often written up in reports so that others can read them. That's why writing skills are essential.

Try This Case

Suppose you are in the police headquarters on the evening of May 4th. The following call comes in:

"Police? This is George Larson of 201 North Division Street. My apartment's been burglarized. The TV, a diamond ring, and 500 dollars in cash are gone. My wife and I just came home from the movies and found our room a mess."

When you go to the apartment, this is what you see:

While you are on the scene, a neighbor, Helena Gomez, says that she saw a man in a dark shirt and dark pants standing in the alley near the fire escape. He seemed to be carrying something heavy.

Words to Know

Complainant — the person who reports the crime

Illegal — against the law

Offense — an illegal act

Suspect — the person who may have committed the crime

Witness — a person who has information about what happened

Tips

on Getting the Facts

When police officers get the facts of a crime, they use the five *W's* and one *H*.

- *Who* was involved?
- *What* happened?
- *When* did it happen?
- *Where* did it happen?
- *Why* did it happen?
- *How* did it happen?

Use the five _W's_ and one _H_ to write a report of the crime.

1. Use the form below. Your report should be clear, accurate, and complete. Include all the facts you can observe.

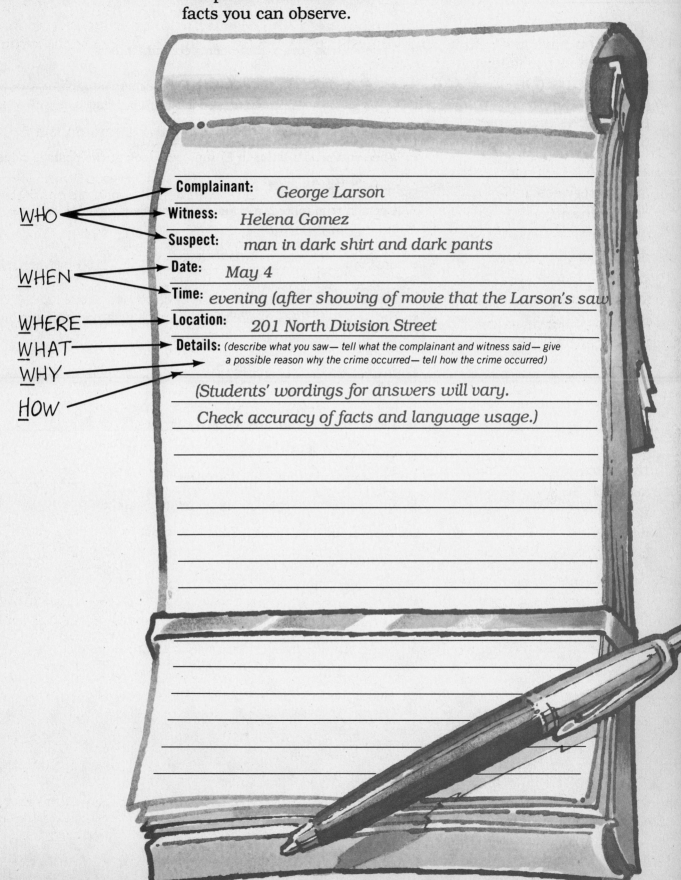

WHO

WHERE
WHAT
WHY

HOW

Complainant: George Larson

Witness: Helena Gomez

Suspect: man in dark shirt and dark pants

Date: May 4

Time: evening (after showing of movie that the Larson's saw)

Location: 201 North Division Street

Details: (describe what you saw — tell what the complainant and witness said — give a possible reason why the crime occurred — tell how the crime occurred)

(Students' wordings for answers will vary.

Check accuracy of facts and language usage.)

Vocabulary Review

1. You have just learned how the following words are used in government jobs. Now use these words to complete the sentences.

airmail
armed services
complainant
detectors
domestic
expert
fatalities
illegal
index
international
jargon
offense
prevention
recruit
reference
suspect
toxic
witness

a. A person who sees a crime being committed is a _____*witness*_____ .

b. People die from _____*toxic*_____ gases as well as from fire itself.

c. When you send a letter to Europe, you look at the postage rates for _____*international*_____ mail.

d. A person who reports a crime to the police is called a _____*complainant*_____ .

e. Most fire _____*fatalities*_____ occur when people are asleep.

f. The _____*armed services*_____ include army, air force, navy, and marines.

g. Smoke _____*detectors*_____ can give early warning of a fire.

h. A letter mailed from Miami to Los Angeles is considered _____*domestic*_____ mail.

i. A new person in the armed services is a _____*recruit*_____ .

j. Almanacs, encyclopedias, and directories are all _____*reference*_____ materials.

110

Reading Skills Review

You have learned how reading skills are used in government jobs. Now use your reading skills to do the following exercises.

1. Complete the statements about parts of an index.

a. Index entries are in _____ *alphabetical* _____ order.

b. The numbers are _____ *pages* _____ where the entry is mentioned.

c. The entry *Congress* is the _____ *main* _____ topic.

d. There are seven _____ *subtopics* _____ under *Congress*.

2. Read the excerpt from a fire department guide at the bottom of the page. Then answer the questions.

a. What is the subject of the guide?
How to escape in case of fire

b. What is the main idea of the second paragraph?
Smoke is your worst enemy.

c. If you are caught in smoke, what should you do?
Get down and crawl toward a window or safe exit.

d. What is the main idea of the last paragraph?
In case of fire, use the stairs, not an elevator.

> ● When fire breaks out, can you escape? This guide will help you escape from homes or high-rise buildings during a fire.
>
> ● Smoke is your worst enemy. It can choke and kill you after a few breaths. If you are caught in smoke, get down and crawl.
>
> ● The elevator is another enemy. It can trap you. If the elevator's signals are triggered by heat, it can get stuck on the fire floor. You wouldn't want to be inside. Always remember where the exit stairs are. Use them to get below the fire floor.

INDEX

Blair, Montgomery, 16
Brademas, John, 106, 108-109
Brown, Henry, 183
Buchanan, James, 85

Carey, Hugh, 132-133
Census, Bureau of, 99
Central Intelligence Agency
 (CIA), 26
China, U.S. relations with, 73
Chisholm, Shirley, 91-92, 95
Civil Service Commission, 46, 55
Civil War, U.S., 14-19
Cleveland, Grover, 85
Coast Guard, U.S., 51
Commerce, Department of, 49
Committee on Committees, 132
Congress
    citizen influence on, 145-149
    and Constitution, 92-93, 95
    enacting a law in, 106-111
    and honesty, 140
    and political parties, 127
    and Presidential power, 57-61
    seniority, system of, 125-126

3. Read the postage rate table below. Then answer the questions.

a. How much postage would you need to send a three-ounce paper by first-class mail?
65 ¢

b. How much would you save if you sent it by third-class mail?
none

Class	1st Oz.	Each Add'l Oz.
First	25 ¢	20 ¢
Third	25 ¢	20 ¢ (up to 4 oz.)

Writing Skills Review

1. Read the following facts. Then use the five *W*'s and one *H* to help you fill out the written report.

Suppose you're a police officer on patrol on March 30 at 10:30 p.m. You spot a man lying on the sidewalk at the northwest corner of Broad and Main. He tells you he was just hit on the head by a man he describes as wearing a black windbreaker. He says the assailant also robbed him of his watch and wallet containing 150 dollars in cash, his driver's license, and three credit cards. The victim gives his name as Ernest Miller of 23 Chestnut Street. You take him to the hospital, where he is found to have bruises on his head and right arm. Later, you continue your patrol of the vicinity around the scene of the crime. During this time, you see a man in a black windbreaker hiding in a doorway. You pick him up as a suspect. His name is Harold Casey and his address is 267 Plymouth Avenue. He has 150 dollars in cash, in his pocket.

(Students' wordings for answers will vary. Check accuracy of facts stated, as well as language usage.)

Unit 8

New Jobs/
New Technology

What will the job market be like when you graduate? The word that best describes the job market is "Change." New jobs are being created. Old jobs are changing. It's hard to think of a job that hasn't been changed in some way by computer technology. What new jobs have computers created? What do people in computer jobs do? What skills do they have? What training should you get to get into a computer-related field? Where are these jobs? When you finish working on this unit, you will be able to answer these questions.

Electronics Technician

Knowing Your Own Interests and Abilities

Is there an electronics technician's job in your future? To help you decide if this job or any job is right for you, you have to know something about the job. You have to know a lot about yourself, too. Then you can judge whether you and a particular job are a good match. Here is the job description.

Job Title: ELECTRONICS TECHNICIAN

1. **Traits and Skills**
   - Good with hands
   - Good at detail
   - Ability to follow directions
   - Enjoy working independently
   - Precision
   - Good eyesight; not color blind

2. **Job Responsibility**
   - Building electronics boards for microcomputers and other electronic products

3. **Training**
   - 18 months post-high school
   - Study of electricity and electronics

4. **Related Careers**
   - Air conditioning and refrigeration servicing (9-month course)
   - Electronics servicing (12-month course)
   - Electronics engineering associate (24-month course)

5. **Where to Find Jobs**
   - Electronics manufacturers
   - Federal government

Words to Know

Electronics — a science that has made possible the development of television, radio, radar, and computers

Engineering — science or work that deals with planning and building engines, machines, roads, etc.

Microcomputers — small, personal-size computers

Precision — being correct or exact

Technician — a person skilled in a certain kind of work

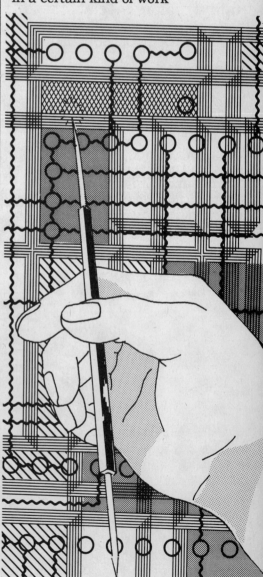

Know Yourself

● Learn to know yourself. What are you good at? What are you not so good at or simply not interested in?

1. Fill out the PERSONAL PROFILE CHART. Then use it throughout this book to see how your personality and skills match a particular job. Put a check in the box that comes closest to telling how you rate for that item. **E** means "excellent," **B** means "good," **F** means "fair."

(Answers will vary.)

PERSONAL PROFILE CHART

	E	G	F		E	G	F
1. Eyesight				12. Talking to People			
2. Hearing				13. Following Directions			
3. Coordination				14. Organizing Skills			
4. General Health				15. Working with Hands			
5. Grooming				16. Sticking to a Task			
6. Patience				17. Making Good Decisions			
7. Getting Along With Others				18. Judgment			
8. Self-Confidence				19. Artistic Ability			
9. Punctuality				20. Working on Your Own			
10. Responsibility				21. Attention to Details			
11. Self-Discipline				22. Neatness in Work			

Decisions! Decisions!

One of the skills needed in many new technology jobs is the ability to make decisions. Whether you work independently or under close supervision, you will make decisions of some kind every day.

2. Look at each of the 22 items in the PERSONAL PROFILE CHART above. Then decide which of the three headings below is right for each item. Write the number of each item under the right heading. The first two have been done for you.

(Some items may be listed under two headings.)

Physical Traits

1
2
3
4
5
___
___

Character Traits

6
7
8
9, 10
11
12
17
18, 19

Work Habits

9
10
13
14
15
16
20
21, 22

Computer-Aided Drafter

Art and the New Technology

Do you prefer paint brushes and art classes to test tubes and laboratories? Take heart! There is a place for people with artistic ability in the new technology world of the 90's. One of the ways of putting artistic ability to use is in a job as a **drafter**.
● What on earth is a drafter? To find out, read the job description on the right.

Words to Know

Artistic ability — skill in one of the arts (such as drawing)

Drafting — drawing a sketch or plan

Floor plan — map of a living or working space

Job Title: COMPUTER-AIDED DRAFTER

1. Traits and Skills
- Ability to use computerized drafting systems
- Ability to visualize and create freehand drawings of three-dimensional objects
- Accuracy and neatness in work
- Careful attention to detail
- Some artistic ability (a plus)
- Good eyesight
- Good with hands
- Ability to work as part of a team

2. Job Responsibilities
- Prepares detailed drawings based on sketches and calculations made by engineers, scientists, and architects
- Calculates strength, quality, and cost of materials
- Uses computer-aided systems and electronic drafting equipment to prepare drawings

3. Training
- Specialized training in technical institutes, junior and community colleges, vocational and technical schools
- Training can range from completion of a three-year vocational high-school program (for drafter trainee job) to three-to-four years post-secondary training (for the job as a computer-aided drafter)

4. Related Careers
- Senior drafter
- Junior drafter
- Surveyor

5. Where to Find Jobs
- Engineering firms
- Architectural firms
- Manufacturing industries (aircraft, ship building, electronics)
- Federal and state government

116

Reading a Floor Plan

● To be a drafter, you must be able to understand drawings of plans. Use the floor plan at the right to answer the following questions.

a. Not counting the bathroom, how many rooms does the apartment have?

three (3)

b. What is the length of the kitchen?

14 feet

c. How many windows does the apartment contain?

five (5)

d. How many closets does the apartment contain?

three (3)

e. What is the width of the bedroom?

11 feet

f. What room do you have to walk through to get to the bedroom?

living room

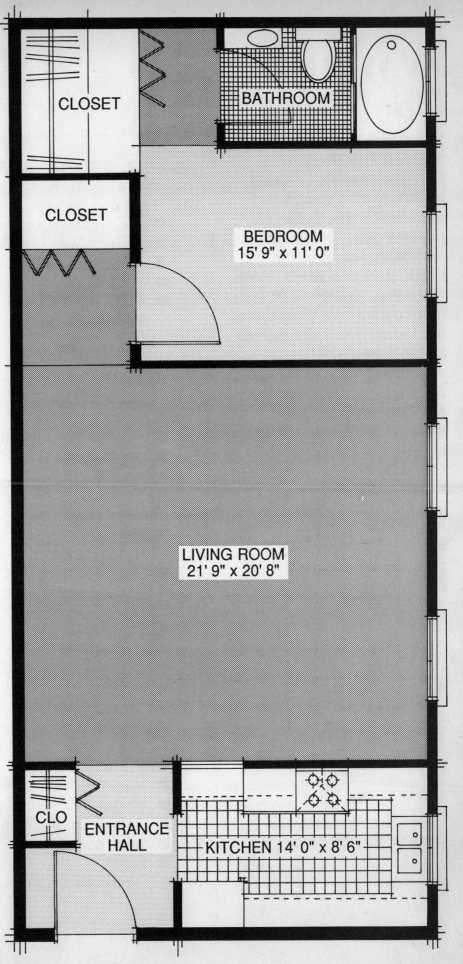

CLOSET

CLOSET

BATHROOM

BEDROOM
15' 9" x 11' 0"

LIVING ROOM
21' 9" x 20' 8"

CLO

ENTRANCE
HALL

KITCHEN 14' 0" x 8' 6"

Computer Operator

The Growing Computer-Related Job Market

Computers are all around us. They are used in manufacturing, in the modern office, in medicine and health care, in the home, and in schools. And tomorrow, there will be more computers than there are today. Does the growth in the number of computers affect the job market? It certainly does! More computers mean more jobs for people who are trained to work with computers.

● Is there a job as a computer operator in your future? To help you decide if this job is right for you, read the job description on the right.

Words to Know

Data Processing — the sorting and classifying of information done by a computer

Input — information fed into a computer for processing

Output — information taken out of a computer

Job Title: COMPUTER OPERATOR

1. Traits and Skills
- Ability to think logically
- Ability to work quickly and accurately
- Work well as part of a team
- Possess independent judgment
- Comfortable working with electronic computer equipment

2. Job Responsibilities
- Loading the computer with the correct equipment (tapes, disks)
- Running the computer
- Paying attention to signals from the computer
- Solving problems with the running of the computer

3. Training
- High-school education, training in mathematics and computers
- Post-secondary school training in data processing preferred

4. Related Careers
- Data entry operator
- Data entry supervisor
- Production control clerk
- Tape librarian
- Production control supervisor

5. Where to Find Jobs
- Manufacturing companies
- Wholesale and retail trade establishments
- Data processing companies
- Large corporations
- Banks
- Government agencies

Put the Data Into the Right Sequence

● Probably the most important skill needed by a computer operator is the ability to think logically. One form of logical thinking is being able to understand the sequence of events in a process. In which order must the steps take place for the process to work?

What Are You Inferring?

● Another kind of thinking is the ability to make inferences. You make an inference when you draw a conclusion from information that is not directly stated. For example, if a friend has won all the prizes in science that his or her school offers, you could infer that your friend has a talent for science.

1. The 8 logical steps in data processing are out of order in the list below. Put them into their correct, logical sequence by numbering each step. The first step has been identified for you.

____3____ **a.** Data is prepared for the computer by a data entry clerk.

____1____ **b.** Sales department requests information about a toy rocket.

____4____ **c.** The computer operator supervises the running of the computer.

____2____ **d.** The job is set up and scheduled for processing.

____6____ **e.** A check is made to be sure the sales department will get all the needed information.

____5____ **f.** The computer is loaded with the correct equipment and instructions for the job.

____8____ **g.** The "output" is bound into booklet form if that was requested.

____7____ **h.** The "output" is printed in the form requested by the sales department.

2. Decide which inference, of the three given for each item below, is the most sensible. Put a check mark in the box for the inference you select.

a. You see someone running out of a bank waving a gun and carrying a bulky sack. A bank guard is pursuing the person. The most likely inference would be that:

☑ The person waving a gun, carrying the bulky sack and running has just robbed the bank.

❑ The two people are acting in a movie being made using the bank and the street as the setting.

❑ The person carrying the bag and running is being chased by an insane person dressed in a bank guard's uniform. The running person — waving a gun and carrying a bag — is defending himself.

b. A friend who lives a few blocks away knocks at your door on a rainy night. The friend is dripping wet. The most likely inference would be that:

❑ Your friend fell into a swimming pool.

☑ Your friend walked over in the rain.

❑ Your friend walked too near a lawn sprinkler.

Vocabulary Review

• There are more words or special terms you can learn when you decide to explore the world of computer technology. Right now, you know some common but important words used in computer-related jobs.

1. Match each word or phrase on the left with its meaning on the right. Write the letter for the correct meaning on the given line.

_f_ electronics

_e_ technician

_d_ microcomputers

_a_ drafting

_c_ output

_b_ data processing

a. drawing a sketch or a plan

b. sorting of information done by a computer

c. information taken out of a computer

d. personal-size computers

e. a person skilled in a certain kind of work

f. a science that has made possible the development of computers

• You have become familiar with the parts of the words **technology**, **technologist**, and **technician**. You will be able to figure out the meanings of many other new technology words, as well as some not so new, but useful ones.

tech — skill, art, craft

– **logy**: science, or study of

– **ician**: one who does or is

– **ist**: one who does or is

2. In the given lines below, write the word that will complete each definition.

a. One who performs magic is a _____ magician _____.

b. One who prescribes diets is a _____ dietician _____.

c. One who types is a _____ typist _____.

d. The science of living things (*bio* means *life*) is called _____ biology _____.

e. A person who is a specialist in technology is a _____ technologist _____.

f. A person skilled in the technical details of a certain occupation is a _____ technician _____.

g. Applied science is called _____ technology _____.

h. The science that studies earth (*geo* means *earth*) is called _____ geology _____.

3. Now, use a dictionary to check your answers.

Reading Skills Review

Fact and Opinion
● A fact is something that can be proven to be true.
● Opinions are usually what a person feels, believes or wants to believe. You can often spot an opinion because the words "I think" or "I believe" or "I guess" are used.

1. Decide which statements below are facts and which are opinions. Write **F** on the given line for a fact. Write **O** on the given line for an opinion.

_____O_____ **a.** I think we'll have space stations on the moon by the year 1995.

_____F_____ **b.** The first small pox vaccination was performed in 1796.

_____F_____ **c.** That bottle contains 40 penicillin tablets.

_____O_____ **d.** I believe that technology will ruin the world.

_____O_____ **e.** Nobody will ever be able to cure the common cold ailment.

2. Pick out the interview facts. Answer the following questions by using the information in the interview with Gary. Write your answers in complete sentences on the given lines.

(Students' wordings for answers will vary. Check for accuracy of facts, correctness in spelling and grammar.)

INT: What does your job involve?
GARY: I maintain robots by cleaning them regularly, changing their parts, and repairing them. This way I can head off many breakdowns.
INT: What training did you need for this job?
GARY: Well. I was already working here when robots were brought in. So, I was trained right here in the plant. The robot manufacturer sent in a training team. But now, community colleges and vocational schools offer training programs in operating and maintaining robots.
INT: Are there any special traits or abilities needed to become a robot maintenance technician?
GARY: Like a surgeon, you should be good with your hands and good at details.
INT: Any others?
GARY: You need a lot of patience. You must be able to think logically. And you should have an aptitude for understanding diagrams and detailed drawings.

a. What are the three traits needed to be a robot maintenance technician?
You should be good with your hands and good at details. You must have patience and be able to think logically. And you should have an aptitude for understanding diagrams and detailed drawings.

b. What are two of Gary's responsibilities on the job?
Gary maintains robots by cleaning them regularly, changing their parts, and repairing them.

c. Where did Gary get his training for his job? *He was trained in the plant where he was already working when the robots were brought in.*

Writing Skills Review

1. Before you can be accepted at a school for training in one of the technology careers, you must be able to fill out an application form neatly and clearly. Fill out the sample form on this page.

(Answers will vary.)

XYZ INSTITUTE

(PRINT OR TYPE ONLY)   Date _____

Name of Student _____ Age _____ Phone _____
                          LAST NAME   FIRST

Address _____ City _____ State _____ Zip _____

Date of Birth _____ Social Security No. _____

Single ❑   Married ❑   U.S. Citizen ❑   Native Born ❑   Naturalized ❑

EDUCATION

Name & Address of School	Dates of Attendance	Course	Grad.

WORK EXPERIENCE
(Information requested in this form will be held in strictest confidence.)

Name & Address of Employer	Date of Employment	Duties

REFERENCES

Name & Address	Position

Course of study you wish to pursue: _____

If accepted, when do you wish to enter school?
❑ morning session   ❑ afternoon session   ❑ evening session   Desired Starting Date _____

Applicants should submit with this application a check or money order, payable to XYZ Institute, in the amount of fifty dollars ($50.00) to be applied as registration fee (non-refundable).

I heard of XYZ Institute through the following:

❑ newspaper   ❑ phone book   ❑ counselor   ❑ friends   ❑ other _____

_____
(Signature of Applicant)

FOR OFFICE USE ONLY

Registrar's Recommendations: _____

122

Skills Checklists

Which Reading and Writing Skills Can You Apply on the Job?

Answer this question by writing a check mark (✔) on the given line for each skill that you believe you have mastered. Note the skills that you still need to practice. Review them on the pages indicated on the right of the chart.

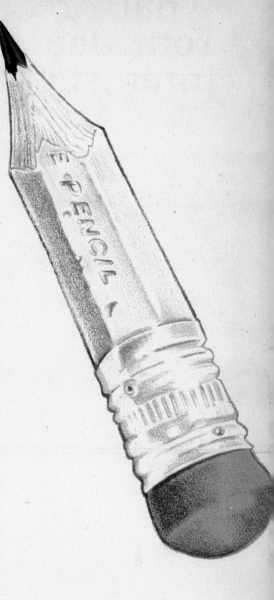

What Are Your Job Interests?

Put a check mark in the box beside the answer that is true for you. Be honest with yourself. This activity is not a test. It is designed to help you look at your job interests. Someday, when the rare moment of choosing between two jobs comes to you, you might take the job that fits many (though not all) of the items you checked.

1. Where would you prefer to work?
❑ outdoors
❑ indoors

2. Which would you like to use most often at work?
❑ mind
❑ eyes
❑ hands
❑ mouth

3. Do you work best with
❑ numbers?
❑ words?
❑ objects (physical things)?

4. Would you prefer to
❑ work closely with others?
❑ work alone?

5. Would you rather be
❑ a leader?
❑ a follower?

6. Which is most interesting to you?
❑ helping other people
❑ doing important work
❑ making money
❑ earning respect from others
❑ having power over others

7. Which description fits your physical condition?
❑ tire easily
❑ able to handle long hours and heavy work

8. When would you prefer to work?
❑ nine to five
❑ night shift
❑ whenever you feel like it

9. Would you
❑ prefer to work near the place where you live?
❑ be willing to move away from home?

10. What kind of career would you prefer?
❑ business
❑ health
❑ agriculture
❑ public service
❑ entertainment
❑ other (specify) _____

Are You Ready for a Job?

Read and answer each question. Put a check mark in the appropriate box for your answer.

Size Up Your Mental Attitudes

	YES	NO
1. Are you ready to take on responsibility for yourself?	❑	❑
2. Can you keep to a regular schedule? (Employers expect employees to get to work on time and to work hard on the job until closing time. You can't be absent or late without a good reason.)	❑	❑
3. Are you ready to take orders, cooperate with others, and act courteously whether or not you feel like it?	❑	❑
4. Are you willing to meet an employer's standard for personal grooming and appearance?	❑	❑

Know the Job Requirements

	YES	NO
1. Do you have the skills required for the job?	❑	❑
2. Should you take certain subjects in high school?	❑	❑
3. Will you need additional schooling in a vocational school or college?	❑	❑
4. Do you need a state license for the job?		
5. Can you get on-the-job training?	❑	❑
6. Will you have to take an examination for the job? (Most government jobs require a Civil Service Examination.)	❑	❑